THE PRIMITIVE MIND-CURE

The Nature and Power of Faith;
Or,
Elementary Lessons in Christian
Philosophy and Transcendental Medicine

With an Essay on
The New Age By William Al-Sharif

By

REV. W. F. EVANS

AUTHOR OF
Mental Cure

First published in 1885

This edition published by Read Books Ltd.
Copyright © 2019 Read Books Ltd.
This book is copyright and may not be
reproduced or copied in any way without
the express permission of the publisher in writing

British Library Cataloguing-in-Publication Data
A catalogue record for this book is available
from the British Library

"To you it is given to know the mysteries of the kingdom of the heavens."

— Mat. xiii : 11.

THE NEW AGE

An extract from the essay,
The New Age by William Al-Sharif

The 'industrial revolution', the 'Enlightenment Age' and colonialism had strengthened the power of the British Empire. Britain, in the second half of the nineteenth century, was probably the most powerful and influential empire in the world. The power of the empire, accompanied with the processes of modernisation and secularisation, created a new religious and cultural mental space. A 'New age' became part of cultural, religious and romantic imaginaire and represented a new era in which religion and culture would evolve in the favour of the empire and its British subjects. In 1843, The New Age was established in London. It proposed a society 'for the promotion of humanity and abstinence from animal food'. This society would also disseminate 'correct principles on universal peace, [and] health of soul and body'.

Christianity, in the age of the empire and missionary expansion, was influenced by the cultural aspirations for a 'new age'. Christian thinkers began to talk about a new age for 'the Lord' and Christianity. This 'new age' would fulfil biblical prophecies and embody new opportunities and truths for the Christian faith. Rationalist intellectuals imagined a new age for progress and science.

The philosophical and scientific criticism of Christianity, the elaboration of 'holistic' practices and theosophical ideas, the British colonialism of India and romantic Orientalism had all provided an inventive climate for the promotion of spiritualistic ideas. The process of modernisation and secularisation diminished the traditional authority of social and religious structures and shaped the transformation from the idea of destiny to choice and from providence to progress. Yet, there were individuals who opposed the religious hegemony of missionary societies and the hierarchal 'church religion' and sought spirituality in holism, occultism and esotericism. The individualised conquest of spirituality, which later influenced the New Age discourse, was formulated by modernism which invented 'the conception of a unique self and private identity, a unique personality and individuality, which can be expected to generate its own unique vision of the world'.

In the US, the 'New Age' imaginaire represented a new spiritual consciousness of the human self and was transformed by the ideas of Spiritualism, Transcendentalism, New Thought, Theosophy and Millenarianism. People such as Woodbury Melcher Fernald (1813-1873) and Warren Felt Evans (1817-1889) spoke of the coming of 'new age' spirituality. A weekly journal, New Age, was issued in San Francisco in 1865. The foundation of the Theosophical Society in 1875 in New York was significant for articulating theosophical concepts. This Society, which established its international headquarters in India, romanticised the religions of India and declared to challenge dogmatic religious authority and scientific materialism.

Despite the emergence of Christian evangelism and fundamentalism, the first three decades of the twentieth century witnessed numerous attempts by 'spiritual seekers' to create new spiritualities and seek new 'truths' for the 'new age'. Henry Jenkins says that the period between 1910 and 1935 was 'the first new age' and 'the period of emergence'.

PREFACE.

This volume is designed to contribute something toward supplying the demand in the public for further light on the subject upon which it treats, — the cure of disease in ourselves and others by mental and spiritual agencies. The first work of the author having a relation to the subject, was published over twenty-two years ago. It was followed, at intervals of different length, by four other volumes, which have had an extensive circulation in every part of the country, and to some extent in Europe. It is not an incredible supposition that they have had an influence, more or less, towards generating in the public mind the widely-spread and growing belief of the mental origin of disease, and of the relation of the mind to its cure. The work is intended to take the reader up where the last volume of the author, "The Divine Law of Cure," leaves him, and conduct him still further along the same path of inquiry. It does not claim to have exhausted the subject, or to have said all that might be said; for the subject is one too vast to be crowded into so limited a compass, which would be like condensing the ocean into the dimensions of a lake. But it is to be hoped that enough has been said to vindicate the propriety of the title, — that of

PREFACE.

"*Elementary* Lessons in Christian Philosophy and Transcendental Medicine." It was our aim to furnish the teachers and pupils of the spiritual philosophy of healing, with a text-book which should elevate the subject into the dignity of a science. The themes discussed are occasionally of an abstruse nature, but have been expressed in the clearest language at our command. It is not intended to wholly supplant the living teacher, but rather to aid his work by suggesting many things it does not say. The work is written also in the interest of self-healing, and contains the essential features of the instruction which the author has given to numerous persons during the last twenty years. There is a large number of people in the world whose life has been a perpetual struggle with disease, and who have been able to discover no pathway of light that unerringly conducts them out of their troubles. The various systems of materialistic medication have been successively tried, and all have failed. To them the volume is sincerely commended and respectfully dedicated, with the hope that they may find in it somewhere the saving power of the right word at the right time. There is in the minds of men, at the present day, an inward thirst, an unsatisfied craving for spiritual light. We wish it was in our power to fully meet this heart-felt want. But we can only promise, in the following pages, to bring to you, "in the name of a disciple," a single cup of water, while we point you to the inexhaustible fountain whence all living, saving truth flows, — the universal Christ, the boundless, everywhere-present realm of pure spirit. Standing by this fountain and well of living water, on which God has never placed a seal, nor stationed around it an armed guard, we would say, in the language of the sublimest of the old prophets, "Ho, every one that thirsteth, come ye to the waters, *and he that hath no money;* come ye, buy and eat; yea, come, buy wine and milk, without money and without price." (Isa. lv : 1.)

For, surely, spiritual truth ought not to be classed among the luxuries which a poor man cannot afford to buy, but rather among the commonest necessaries of life, as air and water, which the Supreme Goodness has scattered, with amazing and beneficent profusion, all over the world, and placed within the reach of all. Of the true water of life, the old symbol of spiritual truth, God has opened a fountain in the inmost region of our own being, and which springs up into everlasting life, if we only knew it. To convince the reader of this will be one of the aims of the present volume. If we succeed in doing this, the book itself will no longer be needed. For when we find the Christ within, "in whom are hid all the treasures of wisdom and knowledge," we have access to more of life and light than all the libraries of the world can give us. When the reader shall have made the grandest discovery ever made in our earthly existence,— the finding of his true *self*, and has identified it with the Christ, of whom it is but a personal limitation,—we will gladly step down from the platform of the teacher, and take our place by your side as a fellow-disciple or pupil. We will no longer open our mouth to speak, but open the inner ear to receive the deep and calm revealing. The education of the future will be a system more in harmony

PREFACE.

with the true meaning of the word, — an educing or guiding out of what is already in us in a state of latency. Spiritual and saving truth is not a foreign exotic which has to be imported from abroad, but is a divine plant, with both flower and fruit, which exists as in its native habitat, in the inmost soul of every man. The signs of the times point unerringly to the coming of a fuller recognition of this ancient truth, and it is the faint light in the east, indicating the approach of a better day for humanity. There are, within the enclosure of our inner being, certain dormant, because unused, spiritual energies and potencies that can save the soul and heal the body of its maladies. To guide these out into conscious and intelligent action, is the end we shall keep steadily in view in these elementary lessons in transcendental philosophy. We have endeavored to restore the ancient doctrine of faith to its primitive meaning, as a saving, healing power. How far we have succeeded, we must leave the reader to judge.

3 BEACON STREET, BOSTON, Dec. 25, 1884.

CONTENTS.

CHAPTER I.
What are Ideas, and What is Idealism? 1

CHAPTER II.
The Application of the Idealistic Philosophy to the Cure of Mental and Bodily Maladies, ... 10

CHAPTER III.
The Triune Constitution of man and the Discovery of the True Self, ... 18

CHAPTER IV.
The Saving Power of the Spirit of Man, ... 29

CHAPTER V.
Happiness and Health, and Where they are to be found, . 39

CHAPTER VI.
The Real and the Apparent in Thought, or the Impossible and Contradictory to Sense is True to the Spirit, . . . 47

CONTENTS.

CHAPTER VII.

Disease Exists only in the Mind on the Plane of Sense, which is the Region of Deceptive Appearances, ... 55

CHAPTER VIII.

The Deepest Reality of Disease is a Morbid Idea and Belief, . 63

CHAPTER IX.

The Science of Oblivescence, or the Art of Forgetting a Malady, 71

CHAPTER X.

The Incipient Idea of Recovery and Whence Does it Come? . 79

CHAPTER XI.

What is it to be Spiritual, and, How may we Become so? . 90

CHAPTER XII.

Spiritual Truth the Best Remedy for Disease, ... 100

CHAPTER XIII.

On the Triune Nature of Man, and the Freeing the Soul from the Body, ... 109

CHAPTER XIV.

Executing Judgment upon Ourselves, or in Thought Separating Disease from the Real Self, ... 117

CONTENTS.

CHAPTER XV.

The Creative Power of the Ideal, or the Externalization of Thought, ... 123

CHAPTER XVI.

The Nature and Right Use of the Will, ... 129

CHAPTER XVII.

The Universal Life-Principle, and its Occult Properties and Uses, 136

CHAPTER XVIII.

The Universal Ether of Science, and the Æther of the Hermetic Philosophy, ... 142

CHAPTER XIX.

The Mother-Principle of Things, and its Use in Self-Healing, . 148

CHAPTER XX.

The Kabalistic and Messianic Method of Healing, and the One Practised by Jesus the Christ, ... 157

CHAPTER XXI.

The Summit of Christian Knowledge, or the Mystery of the Christ, and its Saving Influence, ... 165

CHAPTER XXII.

The Relation of Jesus to the Christ and to Man, . . . 175

CONTENTS.

CHAPTER XXIII.

The Kabalistic Justice and Paul's Righteousness of Faith. Appendix. The Prayer of Faith that Saves the Sick, or the Healing Power of Spiritual Truth, ... 183

CHAPTER XXIV.

Psychological Telegraphy, or the Transference of Thought and Idea from one Mind to Another, ... 199

CHAPTER XXV.

Resurrection from the Body, or the Liberty of the Sons of God, 209

THE PRIMITIVE MIND-CURE.

CHAPTER I.

WHAT ARE IDEAS? AND WHAT IS IDEALISM?

As idealism in opposition to materialism constitutes the philosophic basis on which the psychological or phrenopathic system of cure rests, it is necessary at the outset of our inquiries to form a clear conception of what is meant by that term. Its principles are unanswerably set forth in the work of Bishop Berkeley, entitled *The Principles of Human Knowledge*, published in the year 1710. The doctrines taught by Berkeley were subsequently presented under modifications by a succession of German philosophers, among whom we prominently name Fichte, Schelling, Hegel, and Schopenhauer.

According to Lossius, "Idealism is the assertion that matter (and consequently the human body) is only a *sensuous seeming*, and that spiritual essences are the only real things in the world." This doctrine was taught by Plato, who derived it from Pythagoras and the occult philosophy of Egypt, Chaldea, and India. It is as old as the human race. From the remotest antiquity, it was taught in the Vedas and in all the Oriental philosophies. Says Krug: "Idealism is that system of philosophy which considers the existent or actual as a mere ideal." The definition of Brockhaus is to the same effect: "Idealism, in antithesis to realism, is that philosophical system which maintains not only that the spiritual or ideal is the original, but that it is the sole ac tuality; so that we can concede to the objects of the senses no more than the character of a phenomenal (or apparent) world, educed by ideal activities." (*Real Encyclopædie*, Eleventh Ed., 1866.) In another place, he defines idealism to be "that philosophical view which regards what is *thought* as alone the actually existent." This is the best definition, and accords perfectly with the teaching of the true idealists of all ages and countries. "Thought," says the Kabala, "is the source of all that is." It is the first Sephira or emanation from God. It is the first begotten, the first-born from the "Unknown." It is the *I Am*, the highest manifestation of God in man, and the most real thing in the universe,—that from which everything springs, and to which in its last analysis it can be reduced.

But it is necessary to inquire into the nature of ideas, and their relation to external things, and all the objects of the sense-world. Says Thomas Taylor, in the introduction to the *Parmenides* of Plato: "To the question, *what kind of things, or beings, ideas are*, we may answer with Zenocrates, according to the relation of Proclus, that *they are the exemplary causes of things which perpetually subsist according to nature*. They are exemplars (or the living patterns or models of things) indeed, because the final cause, or *the good* (the supreme God), is superior to them, and that which is properly the efficient cause, or the demiurgic intellect, is of an inferior ordination. But they are the exemplars of things according to nature, because there are no ideas of things unnatural or artificial; and of such natural things as are perpetual, because there are no ideas of mutable particulars." (*Taylor's Translation of Plato*, p. 254.) This is a comprehensive statement of the nature of the Platonic ideas. According to this view, the *ideal* is the *causal*, as the ideal picture in the mind of the artist is the necessary cause of the picture on the canvas. The latter, though only a resemblance, could not exist without the former, because there can be no resemblance that is not the resemblance of something; no appearance that is not the appearance of something. The architect constructs his house in imitation of a preëxisting model or idea, and, without that idea, it might be anything else, as well as a house. So the tabernacle of Moses was to be built after the pattern shown to him in the Mount. So of every object of nature, and of all that endless variety of things, which belongs to the world of sense, they owe their existence to antecedent ideas, which they represent on a lower plane of being. As ideas are the causes of the existence of all material entities, so they sustain a causal relation to the human body, and all its states of health and disease. If I would be perfectly well in body, I must first form the true idea of myself, such as I really am in spirit (or as Paul would say, in Christ). For Plato teaches that the highest soul of man, the *pneuma* of the New Testament, the Buddhi of the Sanscrit, is the idea or living image of God. If I come to the knowledge of this, — my real and immortal self, — it will act as a cause, and adjust the lower animal soul, and the body in harmony with it. And "our earthly house of this tabernacle" will be constructed after the pattern shown to us in the Mount.

All creation is first in *idea*, and is essentially a generating or begetting. Ideas are conceptions; that is, they are the union of pure intellect, which was viewed in the Hermetic philosophy as masculine, with that spiritual and feminine principle, which may be designated by the general term, feeling. This union is *life* whenever and wherever it is effected. It is represented symbolically by the cross, and is the Kabalistic balance, and they express one of the most comprehensive and far-reaching truths in the whole realm of thought. "There is in everything," says Swedenborg, "the marriage of truth and good," or the conjunction of intellect and feeling. This extends through the universe. It is said in the Sohar, the Book of Splendor, or the teaching of the shining ones (Dan. xii: 3), "When the Most Holy Elder, (or the Ancient of days), hidden in all occultations, willed to create, *he made all things in the form of husband and wife.* (*Idra Suta* [*or Smaller Assembly*], sec. 218.) "*All things appear, therefore, in the form of husband and wife;* were it otherwise, nothing whatever could subsist." (*Idra Suta*, sec. 223.) It is an immutable and eternal truth, and one that is fundamental and universal, that nothing exists or can exist, except by the union of intellectual thought with its corresponding feeling, or their correlatives. And ideas are the only "truly existing things," as they are denominated by Plato. They are the generation or creation of the masculine Intelligence (*Nous*), in union with the feminine Wisdom (Sophia), and they are living, enduring, and divine realities. They result from the union of the intellect and feeling on the higher plane of being, and descending to the lower animal soul plane, they are perceived as what are called external objects.

The union of the intellect and feeling, in order to the existence of a living entity, is a truth with which the ancient wisdom-religion was familiar, but has long since been forgotten. When I think of a triangle, or a circle, the thought conjoins itself with the universal principle of feeling, the mother principle, and an idea is formed or perceived in the mind. This is a living and immortal thing.

Thought and feeling are correlative opposites, like the two poles of a magnet. Each implies the other, and they mutually balance each other, and there is an affinitive attration between them, and a spontaneous tendency to a conjunction and a state of equi-libration. When I think that I am well (which is true of my real being), or form an intellectual conception of any mental or bodily condition, the thought will seek to unite itself with the principle of feeling on the intermediate plane of my mental being, and then it becomes *faith*, and a living inward reality, and the substance or subsistence of things hoped for. And it will tend to translate itself into a corporeal expression.

We are to bear in mind, that as there is a world of phenomena or of material things which are only appearances, so *there is a world of ideas* which sustains a constant creative relation to the world of sense, and without which the latter could not exist any more than there could be a shadow without a substance. This realm of ideas is the subjective and real world. It is the "intelligible world" of Plato, and "the kingdom of the heavens" of which Jesus speaks. Wherever there is a material thing, there is back of it, as its soul and life and *cause*, an idea. All things in the natural world are but representations of things in the realm of ideas. This is the old Hermetic doctrine of correspondence which has been reproduced by Swedenborg. Says the Jewish Kabala, "The lower world is made after the pattern of the upper (or inner) world; everything which exists in the upper world is to be found as it were in a copy upon earth; still the whole is one." (*Sohar*, II., 20, *a*.) This is a fundamental principle in our transcendental philosophy, and must be fully apprehended before we can go any farther. It is the key note of our theosophical system. Just as the soul of man, rather than the body, is the real man, so the world of ideas is the *really existing world*. The external Cosmos is but a resemblance, a representation, an appearance of the higher world to the sensuous mind. The world of ideas is that which was called in the ancient philosophy the macrocosm, or greater world; and the material world, including the human body, which belongs to it and is an image of it, was denominated the microcosm, or lesser world.

Owing to the importance of the subject in its relation to our transcendental science of medicine, or science of mental-cure, and the necessity of starting right, on the principle of the maxim of Pythagoras, that "a good beginning is half way to the end," we pursue our inquiry still further into the nature of ideas.

Ideas are the only objects of vision. In this both Berkeley and Locke, and even Condillac agree. But what is the idea of a thing which is the object of vision? It is the spiritual *form* and reality, of which the so-called external object is the correspondent or appearance. Says a distinguished writer, "Let us suppose a man to look for the first time upon some work of art, as, for example, upon a clock, and having sufficiently viewed it, at length to depart. Would he not retain, when absent, an *idea* of what he had seen? And what is it to retain such an idea? *It is to have a form internal correspondent to the external.*" (*Hermes*, by James Harris, p. 375.) But this internal form is all that the man ever saw, and is all that we ever see in any case. The word *form* comes from a Greek word (ὅραμα), meaning that which is seen. The same is true of the term *idea*. In vision, if there is no idea in the mind, we are blind to the object however perfect may be our organs of sight. If there be an idea of a thing in our mind, there is a vision of it proportioned in intensity to the vividness of the idea. If the internal form reaches a certain degree of clearness, it becomes what we call a sensation. The perception of the form, idea, type, pattern, exemplar, species (or whatever we are pleased to call it), of a thing, is necessary to the vision of it. It is the essential thing in every act of vision. *And the external eye is not absolutely necessary to it.* We see things which have all the marks of reality in dreams, and in states of mental abstraction. This mental form, image, or idea expresses not merely the material shape, but the spiritual nature, essence, and reality of a thing. It is this, and this only, that the mind sees, and of which the soul is cognizant in every act or state of visual perception. It is not a mere symbol, a picture, a mental copy, a representation of the thing, but the *ding an sich*, as Kant would say, the thing itself in its inmost reality, the really existing thing, to use a Platonic expression, of which the so-called material exhibition is only its manifestation on a lower and more imperfect plane of thought. The idea is the living *soul* of the thing; the material phenomenon is the imperfect copy. Ideas are not only the only objects of vision, but as they are the essential reality of things, they are the only objects of knowledge or true science, as was long ago taught by Plato.

We remark still further, that ideas are not mere abstract thoughts, but living and immortal entities; material things are their phenomena or appearances, — the shadow and not the substance. This is directly the opposite of the popular conception and belief. Ideas are the living kernel of things; the material organization is the rough shell. When we think of anything, as of Bunker Hill monument, the thought takes form in an idea. This is the thing itself, and more real than the granite rock. It is the only visible entity. Ideas may be defined to be the living and fixed forms assumed by thought. All things which exist have had a previous existence in the *unseen and real world of light*, the world of ideas, and after their dissolution they return to that world. When you burn a rose, as the ancient Magi, or Wise Men, affirmed, it is not destroyed or annihilated, but has only passed from the world of sense to the unseen and real world whence it came. This doctrine of preëxistence applies to minerals, plants, animals, and men. They have existed as *ideas* before they had a material manifestation. This is the doctrine of Plato, and the teaching of all the philosophies of the East. It is expressed in unmistakable language in the first chapters of Genesis. "These are the generations of the heavens and of the earth when they were created, in the day when Jehovah God made the earth and the heavens, and every plant of the field before it was in the earth, and every herb of the field before it grew." (Gen. ii : 4, 5.) All things were created in idea and in reality before they were in the earth. Their generation, or incarnation, or descent into matter is to be viewed in the light of a degradation, but one that has its reward, for here they touch the bottom in the descending line of evolution, and begin to rebound on the home stretch, or upward side of the cycle, the ascending and shining way to the blest abodes. Jesus had a glory with the Father before the world was (to him), that is, before his descent into material conditions. So perhaps had we, and all other men, which is one of the oldest doctrines of philosophy, and when properly understood, one of the most rational. Whatever is true of Jesus in that respect, is true of man.

Ideas are but poorly expressed in the deceptive and illusory world of sense. The objects of nature are not truly existing things, but are only in a state of *becoming*, that is, they exhibit an effort to realize the ideal plan of their being. In illustration of this, take the geometrical figures, as a line, a triangle, a circle. There is not a perfect circle in the whole material universe. There can be only a resemblance of one. But there is a circle, real, perfect, and eternal in the world of ideas, which lies above and within this world. So there is in every one of us an *ideal* and immortal man. This is not the dream of a disordered fancy, but a divine reality. There is in us an instinctive striving to climb up to its full realization. To find this ideal man as a fact of consciousness, and recognize it as the living image of God in us and as our *real self*, is the aim we have in view. To release this inward and real self from the bondage of matter, and free it from all material conditions and restraints, is the goal toward which the path on which we now enter conducts our willing feet. Then we are glorified with the glory which we had before the world had an existence in us and for us.

This is not a new doctrine, but belongs to the Platonic philosophy, and is well stated by Plotinus. "May we not say that prior to this subsistence in a state of *becoming*, we *had* a subsistence as men in *true being*, though different men from what we now are, and possessing *a deiform nature?* We were likewise pure souls and intellects conjoined with universal essence, being parts of the *intelligible* (world); not disjoined or separated from it, but pertaining to the whole of it. For neither are we now cut off from it. For even now the man that is here wishing to be another man, accedes (or approaches in thought) to the man that is there, and which, finding us (for we are not external to the universe), surrounds us with himself, and conjoins himself to that man which each of us then was. Just as if one voice and one discourse existing, some one from a different place applying his ears should hear and receive what was said, and should become in energy a certain hearing, in consequence of having that which energizes present with itself. After the same manner we become both the man which is in the intelligible (or ideal world) and the man which is here." (*Translations from the Greek of some Treatises of Plotinus,* by Thomas Taylor, p. 41.)

This is only the soul or *psychical* man, uniting itself to the inward divine *pneuma* or spirit. The two extreme links of the chain of our being are brought together in a circle, and man in the discrete degrees of his existence is made a completed unity. The ideal and immortal man, which is latent in most, becomes the actual and conscious man. This is salvation in the Pauline and true Christian sense, but is a conception which belongs to a spiritual philosophy that had an existence in ages long anterior to the advent of Christianity.

CHAPTER II.

THE APPLICATION OF THE IDEALISTIC PHILOSOPHY TO THE CURE OF MENTAL AND BODILY MALADIES.

THE philosophy of idealism as presented in the preceding lesson is to be applied to the cure of disease, as it was by Jesus the Christ. All disease, so far as it has a material or bodily expression, must have had a preëxistence in us as a fixed mode of thought, that is, as an idea. To expunge from the mind and obliterate from our soul-life the idea of it, is to remove the cause of it, and hence to cure the malady. How best to accomplish this is the problem to be solved by our transcendental medical science and practical metaphysics. To its solution we will now devote our best energies.

It is our aim to reproduce the system of cure practiced by Jesus, and adapt it to modern modes of thought and expression. Now Jesus was the prince of idealists, as Keshub Chunder Sen has said, and his religion is supreme idealism. (*Oriental Christ*, by P. C. Mozoomdar, p. 34.) Without a knowledge of the philosophy of idealism it is impossible to comprehend the profound truths of Christianity or any of the Oriental religions. With Jesus, as with Gautama the Buddha, ideal things, existing in a sphere of being interior to the world of sense, were the only real and enduring things. All else was evanescent and ever changing.

We have endeavored to find in the realm of mind certain fixed principles as fundamental, immutably true, and trustworthy as the principles of geometry, by which the mariner guides his course upon the pathless deep. In the New Testament doctrine of faith, as it was viewed by Jesus, and

Paul, and even Plato, we affirm that we have such a principle in its application to the cure of the diseases of the soul and the body. When properly understood we see why, as Jesus declared, it is ever unto us according to our faith (Matt. ix: 29). This is a principle as certain in the laws of mind, and as reliable as that a straight line is the shortest distance between two given points, or the demonstrated theorem that in every right-angled triangle the square of the hypothenuse is equal to the sum of the squares of the other two sides. Faith may be defined to be the power of perceiving spiritual realities that lie above and beyond the range of the senses, and a confidence in those higher truths. This is essentially the definition of it given by the unknown Kabalistic author of the Epistle to the Hebrews (Heb. xi: 1).

Faith is the source of all spiritual power. The end and purpose of all education is, and will be of our present studies, the achievement of spiritual development and the attainment of a truly spiritual mode and habit of thought. In other words, our aim should be expressed in the comprehensive prayer, "Lord, increase our faith" (Luke xvii: 5). This implies that we already have faith in a degree, which only needs to be augmented and turned in the right direction. On this subject Mr. A. P. Sinnett very justly remarks: "One may illustrate this point by reference to a very common-place physical exercise. Every man living, having the ordinary use of his limbs, is qualified to swim. But put those who cannot swim, as the common phrase goes, into deep water, and they will struggle and be drowned. The mere way to move the limbs is no mystery; but unless the swimmer in moving them has a full belief that such movement will produce the required result, the required result is not produced. In this case we are dealing with mechanical forces merely, but the same principle runs up into dealings with subtler forces." Of the power which resides in faith, he gives as instances the marvels wrought by the genuine

Oriental adepts. Their training is designed to develop the principle of faith. (*Esoteric Buddhism*, p. 12.) Read also on the same subject the eleventh chapter of the Epistle to the Hebrews. But every one will ask, "How may we get this faith?" In this case the questioner is like the man who is anxiously hunting around the house to find his spectacles, but all the time has them on and is looking through them. We already have faith, and are perpetually acting under its influence and guidance, but have not learned its higher applications and uses. Faith is only that intuitive intellectual perception that lies above the range of the sensuous plane of the mind's action, and which we call into exercise every time we correct the illusions of our senses, and judge and act contrary to their deceptive appearances. Whenever we judge, not according to appearance, but judge righteously or according to a divine rectitude of thought, we exercise faith. When I perceive that the reflected image from a mirror is not a solid object behind the mirror, or that the earth turns on its axis, and that the sun does not rise and set, it is that higher form of knowledge which is called faith.

According to the idealistic philosophy, *thought and existence are absolutely identical and inseparable.* This is a principle as universally true as that two straight lines which are parallel will never meet, however far they may be extended, or the proposition that the whole of a thing is equal to the sum of all its parts. Bishop Berkeley, after remarking that time is nothing abstracted from the succession of ideas in our minds, and that the duration of any finite existence must be estimated by the number of ideas, or actions, succeeding each other in that individual spirit or mind, says: "Hence, it is a plain consequence that the soul always thinks; and, in truth, whoever shall go about to divide in his thoughts, or abstract the *existence* of a spirit from its *cogitation*, will, I believe, find it no easy task." (*Principles of Human Knowledge*, sec. 98.)

Pure thought is the summit of our being. It is the Kabalistic Crown, and is spirit; and, by divine appointment, governs and controls all below it. It is the point where our individual existence flows out from the "Unknown." The attainment of the power to think spiritually and spontaneously, in contradistinction from the possession of a set of borrowed opinions, is the "crown of life." Since to think and to exist are one and the same, a man in whatsoever condition he is, whether in health or disease, whether happy or the opposite, is only the *expression* or external translation of his thoughts and ideas. He is the perpetual creation of his fixed mode of thought. The world and all the things it contains, including the body of man, having no thought in themselves, do not exist in and for themselves, but exist only in us, and as Schopenhaur has truly said, are to us only what we *think* and *believe* them to be. As thought and existence are identical, a change of thought must necessarily modify our existence. To *think* a change in our bodily condition, and not merely to think about it, will determine all the living forces toward that result, as certainly as a stream issuing from a fountain will flow in another direction when we change the direction of its channel.

If thought is the first act of our individual spiritual existence, and a perpetual concomitant of it, and is the primal force and most subtle energy in the universe, the question will arise, is thought free and subject to no law above itself? Can we think when and what we please? In disease, can I think that I am well? In pain, can I think that I have no pain? I answer unhesitatingly, I can. All things are possible to thought. I can *think* that five plus four is twelve, but may not be able to *believe* it until the thought is joined with feeling in some degree. A man may think that his dwelling is on fire when it is not, and he is affected by it; or he may think that his house is not on fire when it is, and in the latter case he feels no alarm. In both cases his thought modifies his existence. A man may think he is dying when he is not; or, when he is passing through what the world calls death, he may both think and *feel* that it is only a higher form of life, and that there is no death. In sickness, it is possible to think, and even believe, that the disease does not belong to the class of *truly existing things*, but is only a phenomenon or appearance, a false seeming, an illusion. This thought maintained will vindicate its right to be called the Crown by transforming all below it into its expression. Thought may be subject to certain laws or fixed rules of action, as may be predicated of the Divine nature itself, but is absolutely free; for the laws of its activity arise from its own essence. It knows no higher law than itself. Pure thought is the first emanation from God, as is seen in the Kabalistic scheme of the Ten Sephiroth. It is not a mere attribute or faculty of spirit; it is spirit itself. We cannot abstract thought from spirit any more than a smile can be separated from a human face, and left as an entity in empty space; and the spirit as the first emanation from God, as the Kabala affirms, is the Son of God. And as the Father has life in himself, so he has given to the Son (or the spirit) to have life in himself; and he gave him authority also *to execute judgment* because he is also the son of man. (John v : 26, 27.) The essential characteristic of spirit, and which inheres in its very essence, as Hegel has said, is freedom and spontaneity. It *originates* action or motion, as Plato teaches. The essential property of matter is passivity or fatality. Thought is not like the vane on the church tower, turning in every direction from the action of a force existing outside of itself. But the spirit is a wind or breath of God that bloweth where it listeth. (John iii : 8.) It chooses its own direction in which to act. There is nothing above it but the "Unknown God," out of whom it perpetually springs. As the sun is never separated from any of his rays, but acts as one with each and all of them, so the "Father of spirits" always approves and sanctions the action of pure spiritual thought. For pure thought is the Protogonos, the first begotten, the son and perpetual offspring of God, and from him it is never sundered. If thought and existence are identical, then it follows that to think rightly is to be well and happy. All matter including the human body exists only in mind, which is the only *substance*. It exists from thought and in thought. Hence, the body is to me, and for me, what I *think* it to be. This is an absolute and irrepealable law of our being, as much so as that all right-angled triangles are equal to each other, or that every circle, great or small, contains three hundred and sixty degrees. How soon a change of thought and feeling, as in passing from melancholy to cheerfulness, translates itself into a bodily expression! So when doubt and despair give place to hope and the full assurance of faith, the change expresses itself immediately in the face, which is the index of our interior states of mind and body. Behold in this the creative omnipotence of thought and feeling. Thought and feeling are the Elohim, the *Dii Potentes*, the creative potencies in our microcosm or lesser world, as they are in the macrocosm or greater world of ideas, and they are continually saying in us, "Let us make the body after our image and likeness." In the above short sentence, as in a casket, lies the golden key which unlocks the mysteries of health and disease.

That which we most need is to develop into consciousness our inner and higher life, and to give to it what rightfully belongs to it — an absolute sovereignty over all below it. It should be our aim to elevate the principle of thought above the plane of the senses, and free it from their distorting influences. "This elevation above sensual things was known to the ancients, and their wise men said that when the mind is withdrawn from sensual things, it comes into an interior light, and, at the same time, into a tranquil state, and into a sort of heavenly blessedness. Man is capable of being yet more interiorly elevated; and the more interiorly he is elevated, into so much the clearer light does he come, and at length into the light of heaven, which is nothing else but wisdom and intelligence from the Lord." (*Arcana Celestia*, 6313.) As thought becomes more internal, or elevated above the body and the external senses, it becomes more potential. This is the true meaning of healing ourselves or others. It is the emancipation of the soul from material thraldom. And, when the soul is saved from its illusions, the body can well be left to take care of itself. Says Paul: τὸ δὲ φρόνημα τοῦ πνεύματος ζωὴ καὶ εἰρήνη, the thought of the spirit is life and peace; but the thought of the fleshly mind (or the habit of thinking on a level with the body), is death. (Rom. viii : 6, 7.) This passage contains, in a small compass, the true philosophy of salvation in the full sense of the word. It will be our work to develop this living germ and fruitful seed of truth into a tree whose leaves shall be for the healing of the nations.

We encounter at the outset in our instruction a great evil, and one that has served to hold humanity down and prevent its rising from the plane of sense to the life of faith. I refer to the fact that the church, Catholic and Protestant, has claimed a monopoly of the principle of faith. They have connected it with certain dogmas which are, to many intelligent minds, unreasonable, absurd, and incredible. They have enclosed the divine and saving principle of faith in what looks to many as an unseemly wrapper, like the precious goods of the merchant in coarse paper, and they refuse to deliver the merchandise unless you take it in the unsightly wrapper. The invalid or sinner (as the case may be) desires to be healed or saved, and works himself into a willingness to take the standard theological medicine as the less of two evils, but he cannot avoid saying (or at least thinking) with Whittier : —

THE PRIMITIVE MIND-CURE.

> "I trace your lines of argument;
> Your logic linked and strong
> I weigh as one who dreads dissent,
> And fears a doubt as wrong.
>
> But still my human hands are weak
> To hold your iron creeds;
> Against the words ye bid me speak
> My heart within me pleads."

But, at the present time, many people are beginning to feel that they can buy directly of the Christ "gold tried in the fire," and enclose the celestial and enduring good in their own theological envelope. Faith is a philosophical and scientific principle much older than even Plato, and belongs, by just right, as an exclusive property to no one sect, but to all mankind, as much so as the light of the sun. In these lessons we shall try and put you in possession of this "pearl of great price," and leave you to find your own casket. I can but feel that those persons in the various churches who have unselfishly devoted themselves to the practice of the faith cure, and who include in their number many of the choicest spirits on earth, would find their success still greater if they could divorce more fully the saving principle of faith from un-Christian and mentally unwholesome theological dogmas. In other words, let us give allopathic prescriptions of pure religion, but infinitesimal doses of the popular theology. It is to be hoped this suggestion will be taken in the spirit in which it is given; for, as one has beautifully said:—

> "A bending staff I would not break,
> A feeble faith I would not shake,
> Nor even rashly pluck away
> The error which some truth may stay,
> Whose loss might leave the soul without
> A shield against the shafts of doubt."

CHAPTER III.

THE TRIUNE CONSTITUTION OF MAN AND THE DISCOVERY OF THE TRUE SELF.

It is the object of these lessons to lead gradually, and by successive steps, to the development of the unexplored, and, in modern times, almost universally unrecognized, but really vast powers for good that belong to a truly religious and spiritual faith — a faith that perceives being in opposition to a mere sensuous and illusory appearance. There is a faith that perceives and consciously recognizes those truths and realities which lie beyond the grasp of the animal or psychical man or mind. In the Sanscrit language, in which is locked up the profoundest truths ever revealed to the human mind, the word for truth is *sat* or *satya*, which is the participle of the verb *as*, to be. Hence, truth is that which *is*, in contradistinction from that which only *seems* to be. It is the τὸ ὄντως ὄν, or truly existing being of Plato; the *amen* of Jesus and Paul. Faith is the perception of these supersensuous truths, and says of them, "these are that which *really is*," and maintains this attitude of thought in opposition to the fallacious and deceptive appearances of the senses.

In order to reach this position of thought, we must first discover our true self. To him who would become spiritual this is of supreme importance. When we discover our *real self*, we find at the same time God, and health, and heaven. In the philosophy of the Vedas, which means real knowledge, all the ordinary names of God, as the Almighty, the Creator, etc., are laid aside, and the single name *Atman*, the Self, is used to denote the divine Being. This does not refer to the *Aditi*, the Boundless, the Absolute Being, which is nameless, but to the highest manifestation of the Supreme Divine Essence. It is the Self, or underlying, or inmost Reality, of all that is. It is the Absolute Self, which includes our individual self in it. The Atman is the Self in which each individual self must find rest, must come to himself, must find his own true self, the immortal *Monad*, the spiritual and imperishable entity. All this teaches the sublime truth of faith, that in our inmost being we become identified with the Divine Nature. The highest wisdom of Greece was expressed in the precept, "know thyself." When we find our real self, everything afterwards in our path is easy. We must, in the outset, as the French would say, find our true East (*s'orienter*), and fix our true position among created things. We must ascertain the direction in which we are to look for spiritual wisdom, and the region of our being where alone it can be found.

In the Vedanta philosophy of India, the oldest religious philosophy of the world, it is said: "There is nothing higher than the attainment of the knowledge of the Self." Again: "Despising everything else, a wise man should strive after the knowledge of the self." This highest Self is called in the Vedanta, which means the end or goal of the Veda, the "silent thinker," as being the inmost spring of all thought. It is also called "the one who knows," as it partakes of the Divine Omniscience. It is also the "old man within," who is identical with the Kabalistic "Ancient of Days," "the holy elder," which means the inward sage, the source of all true knowledge, and fountain of all true wisdom, for at this point it opens into that in which are hid all the treasures of wisdom and knowledge. This inmost *self* in us is a *person* only in the true sense of the word, as a *mask* that conceals and partly reveals the universal spirit. To discover our real self, and to find it included in the being of the manifested God, the Christ of Paul, is the Platonic idea of redemption, and is the summit of all spiritual knowledge. It is faith in its supreme sense.

The Atman of the Vedanta, the highest Self, and the Christ of Paul, the Adam Kadmon of the Kabala, are the same as the "Over-Soul" of Emerson. He says of it: "The Supreme Critic on the errors of the past and the present, and the only prophet of that which must be, is that great nature in which we rest, as the earth lies in the soft arms of the atmosphere; that Unity, that Over-Soul, within which every man's particular being is contained and made one with all others." (*Essays*, First Series, p. 214.)

In another place, speaking of the Over-Soul, Emerson says: "Of this pure nature every man is at some time sensible. Language cannot paint it with his colors. It is too subtile. It is undefinable, unmeasurable, but we know that it pervades and contains us. We know that all spiritual being is in man. A wise old proverb says, 'God comes to see us without bell'; that is, as there is no screen or ceiling between our heads and the infinite heavens, so is there no bar or wall in the soul where man, the effect, ceases, and God, the cause, begins. The walls are taken away. We lie open on one side to the deeps of spiritual nature, to the attributes of God." (*Essays*, First Series, p. 216.)

The importance of finding this higher self, and developing it into consciousness, cannot be overstated. It is necessary to all spiritual growth. It has always been earnestly insisted upon by all who have written anything on the deeper philosophy of human nature. The celebrated Arabian philosopher, Muhammed Al Ghazzali, who was born A.D. 1056, wrote a work entitled *The Alchemy of Happiness*. It contains the principles of a profound spiritual science, the same that were taught under impenetrable symbols by the Alchemists of the middle ages. Al Ghazzali commences his work with these important words, which are the key to all spiritual science: "O seeker after the divine mysteries!

know thou that the door to the knowledge of God will be opened to a man first of all, when he knows his own soul, and understands the truth about his own spirit, according as it has been revealed. 'He who knows himself, knows his Lord also.' Again, in the books of former prophets it is written, 'Know thine own soul, and thou shalt know thy Lord'; and we have received it in a tradition, 'He who knows himself, already knows his Lord.' This is a convincing argument that the soul (or spirit) is like a clean mirror into which, whenever a person looks, he may there see God." This was written eight centuries ago. But thousands of years before this it was said in the Vedanta of India, "There is one eternal thinker, thinking non-eternal thoughts; he, though one, fulfils the desires of many. The wise who perceive him within their self, to them belongs eternal life, eternal peace." (*India*, by Max Müller, p. 260.)

That man possesses a triune nature, and is capable of living and acting on either of three distinct planes of being, or, as it is stated in the spiritual philosophy of Swedenborg, that there are three discrete degrees of the mind, is one of the oldest doctrines of philosophy, but is wholly unrecognized in our modern systems of metaphysics. It is a fundamental idea in the New Testament psychology, as also in the philosophy of Plato, and is the key to the theosophical system of the Christ. In the First Epistle to the Thessalonians, Paul gives the Platonic statement of this doctrine: "And the God of peace himself sanctify you wholly, and may your *spirit*, and *soul*, and *body* be preserved whole (or entire) without blame at the appearance of our Lord Jesus Christ." (I Thes. v: 23.) The body is here used for the lowest degree of the mind, the animal nature with the degree of intellect that belongs to it. It is that which is called in the writings of Paul the carnal or fleshly mind. It is the Linga Sharira of Esoteric Buddhism, or what is called the *astral body*. It is of an etherial nature, but not immortal. It belongs to this material stage of our existence, and is that intermediate principle which connects the higher degrees of the mind or thinking substance with matter and with the body.

The lowest degree of our immortal nature is called the animal soul, and is the *psyche* of the New Testament, and constitutes what the Apostle Paul denominates the *psychical man*, which is badly translated "the natural man," which designation of it is followed by Swedenborg. It is the region in us of what is called external sense. It is also the seat of all the animal appetites and passions. As such, it was denominated by Pythagoras *thumos*, and by the Buddhists is called *kama rupa*, or body of desire, and vehicle of will. By the Hebrews it was called *nephesh*, and is the serpent of Genesis, through the influence of which man fell from the spiritual state into which he was created into a sensuous or psychical condition. And as Moses lifted up the serpent in the wilderness on the cross as the Kabalistic tree of life, so must the son of man, or the animal soul, be lifted up. (John iii: 14.) For though humanity, on this plane of mental being, is animal in its nature when compared with spirit, it is elevated above the correctly defined animal creation in every other respect. And though this region is called the animal soul, as it is the highest *developed* principle of the brute creation, it is yet susceptible of evolution into something far higher, by its union with the higher degrees of our being. (*Esoteric Buddhism*, by A. P. Sinnet, p. 25.)

To this region of mind belongs, according to Plato, what we denominate *opinion*, or the reception of the beliefs of others. Opinions may be founded on truth, or they may be false. When true, they come next to knowledge as a practical guide, and as near to genuine faith as the large majority of mankind ever come. Here, also, is what we call reason, which is a much less unerring guide than instinct, which belongs to the animal soul, and which brings us to the boundaries of the next higher degree. Instinct in man and animals is the knowledge that we derive from the Universal Soul or Mind, of which our soul is only a personal limitation, or individual expression. The animal soul is the basement story of our immaterial, intellectual nature. It is the region in us of the evil and the false, of sin and disease; and we must acquire the power of transferring our consciousness to a more internal plane of being.

The next degree or region of the mind is where it rises above the darkness and fallacies of the senses, and thinks and acts on the plane of pure intellect. It is the region of spiritual intelligence in distinction from external science or sensuous knowledge, which belongs to a lower intellectual range. It is called in the Sanscrit *manas*, which is translated human soul, as it is the distinctively human principle, and that which distinguishes man from the highest of the animal kingdom. It has been called also the rational soul, but is more properly designated the intellectual soul, as reason belongs to the psychical man, and never discovers truth. It is a distinct mind, including the intellect and all the emotions and affections that belong to the mind. It is the interior man. Its development into consciousness should be our highest aim. After the *anastasis* of Jesus he appeared to the disciples and opened their understanding (*noema*, not psyche, or animal soul) that they might understand the Scriptures (Luke xxiv: 45). And the psalmist prays: "Open thou mine eyes, that I may see wondrous things out of thy law" (Ps. cxix: 18). This is that region of mind that perceives things in *idea*, and consequently independently of the senses. Its range of vision is well-nigh unlimited. In this region of our being the divine omniscience comes to the dawning in us. Of the state of intellectual lucidity and spiritual vision that is natural to this degree of the mind, Paul speaks as "having the eyes of the understanding enlightened" (Eph. i:18). And he prays that the Colossian Christians might be filled with the knowledge of God's will in all wisdom and spiritual understanding or discernment (Col. i:9). The intellectual soul is a region of mental elevation, or rather inwardness, where man is no longer blinded by the external senses, but where the higher perceptive faculties act independent of all organic instruments. It is what Swedenborg inaccurately denominates the *spiritual* man, though he properly apprehends and describes this state of man.

It is proper to remark that this distinct region of mind and higher story or plane of our being is the seat of faith, which is the perception of truth lying above the range of the senses. It is the location in us, so to speak, of the higher senses and of ideas. In it also is found conscience, of which animals are destitute. In it we perceive *reality*, the *rita* of the Sanscrit, which answers to the Kabalistic *justice* and Paul's "righteousness of faith," which signifies the perception of real truth in opposition to the illusions of the senses.

As the intellectual soul is the real man, and is capable of thinking and acting independent of both time and space, which are not external to it, but only modes and states of thought, it can transfer its real presence and personality to any place however remote. As in this degree of our being we begin to partake of the divine omniscience, so also we begin to share the divine omnipresence. It is this principle in us, when conjoined with the more subtle elements of the animal soul, that is capable of going where it pleases, and of actually appearing to distant persons, and speaking to the inward ear, as we read of the Hindu adepts. This is done by them by the application of certain mental forces and spiritual laws, a knowledge of which can be acquired. This occasionally takes place with persons at the hour of death, but could be done as well before this if we learn to free the interior man from the trammels of the body. Swedenborg affirms from his own experience that the spaces and distances, and consequent progressions or movements which exist in the natural world are, in their origin and first cause, only changes of the state of interior things; in other words, of thought and feeling. And man, as to his spirit, is capable of translation to any distance, while the physical body continues in its own place. (*Earths in the Universe*, sec. 125.)

The *pneuma* or spirit is the supreme degree of the mind or thinking principle, — the dome of the temple of God in man, where our being rises into the immeasurable heavens. The *pneuma* of Jesus and Paul is the inmost degree of the mind, the angelic and divine man, the immortal and real self. It is the celestial range of the mind's activity, and the seat of the divinest powers and capabilities of human nature, since, as Jesus declares, "God is Spirit," man as *a* spirit comes into close relationship to the Godhead. Says Philo, the mystic Alexandrian Jew, in a letter to Hephæstion, "God has breathed into man from heaven a portion of his own divinity. That which is divine is invisible. *It may be extended, but is incapable of separation.* Consider how vast is the range of thought over the past and the future, the heavens and the earth. This alliance with an upper world, of which we are conscious, would be impossible were not the soul (spirit) of man an indivisible portion of that divine and blessed Soul." The spiritual degree of the mind is the divine realm of our being where the boundary line that distinguishes our individual existence from the Godhead is obscurely marked, so that where the one ends and the other begins can with difficulty be discerned. Here each one of us is a finite limitation of the universal spirit, but not separate from it, as the air in this room, though a distinct portion of the boundless atmosphere, is not sundered from it. From this inmost depth of his conscious life Jesus, speaking for all men, said, "I and my Father are one"; and his being became so intermingled with that of God that he could say, "The Father is in me, and I am in the Father."

"The spirit," says Dr. Wyld, "is the third factor in the triune man. It is that which is an atom or spark of the spirit of God. It is the hidden centre or 'light of every man that is born into the world,' and hidden from the foundation of the world. It is the secret Logos, which became effulgent in Jesus, and it is that by which only God can be known. It is above and beyond reason. It is the nature of the knowledge and wisdom and power of God." (*Theosophy and the Higher Life*, p. 12.)

This region of our being was denominated by Pythagoras, the *Nous*, pure intelligence. In it faith becomes intuition, its highest form. It is that immaterial and immortal substance, or essence, that is called in the German, *geist;* in the French, *esprit;* and in the New Testament, *pneuma*. But the Sanscrit designation of it as *buddhi* is the most expressive of all the names given to it in the various languages. This means about the same as the inward Christ of Paul. It is the Christ principle within, and the only hope of glory. Its development in us, from its latent state into consciousness, is eternal life. For this region of the real self is never diseased or unhappy, and never dies. "It is only the finite that suffers," says Emerson; "the infinite lies stretched in smiling repose."

The spirit in man is the "Son of God" of which Paul and the Kabala speak. It is also the "inward voice," the Metatron, the redeeming angel. This still small voice is the *Vach*, the sacred speech, the unutterable word of the occult philosophy. This is resident in the hidden depths of our own being, and in its reality always comes from within, and never from without.

It is a great advance in our spiritual development, and an important point gained toward the attainment of a mental power to cure disease in ourselves or others when we come to a clear perception of the truth that man is already a *spirit*, and not merely sometime to become one. Every man, as to his inner and real self, is as veritable a spirit as he ever will be, only he does not *know* it; and we do not see him as such, because, in our superficial vision, we see only that which hides the real man from our sight.

This is the true *idea* of man; and, when intuitively perceived, the idea, steadfastly maintained, will translate itself into an expression upon every plane of our being. The spirit is the supreme and celestial man; and, by virtue of its divine and immortal nature, it is never diseased or unhappy. It possesses the right of dominion over the lower or outer degrees of our being. It speaks, and it is done; it commands, and it stands fast. It is one of the highest powers in nature because it is divine.

It is proper to remark, in closing this explication of the triune constitution of man, that this doctrine is absolutely fundamental, and must be fully apprehended and appropriated, or our progress will hereafter be laborious and difficult. We need so to master this conception of human nature, that we can more or less distinctly define, in our consciousness, the boundaries of these discrete regions of our mental being, so that our varying thoughts and feelings, good or evil, which make up the whole of human life, may be referred to their proper place in us. To assist us in doing this, and to make this desirable attainment easier, and to aid the memory in tenaciously holding this doctrine, we furnish the reader with the accompanying ancient diagram which symbolically represents it to the eye.

TRIUNE MAN.

Nous.
Pure Intelligence.
Inward Voice.
Intuition.
Metatron.
Vach.

Celestial Man.
Spirit.
Pneuma.
Buddhi.
Son of God.
Inward Christ.
Real Self.

Justice.
Faith.
Ideas.
Higher Senses.
Reality.
Conscience.

Intellectual Soul
Logos.
Manas.
Ruach.
Human Soul.

Instinct.
Reason.
Opinion.
Appetites.
Passions.
Seat of Evil.
Sin. Disease.

Animal Soul.
External Sense.
Psyche of N. T.
Kama Rupa.
Nephesh.
Psychical Man.
Thumos.

Matter.
Maia.
Shadow.

Body. Soma.
Rupa.
Unreal Man.

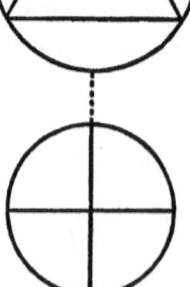

CHAPTER IV.

THE SAVING POWER OF THE SPIRIT OF MAN.

In the region of our own spirit we come into sympathetic and receptive communication with the collective intelligence, or the universal Christ. There is a unity in the sublime life of the spirit that leaves no room for a mere isolated individuality, a mere personal existence sundered from the grand whole. Each discrete region of our being is connected with a universal principle or sphere of existence, of which it is a personal limitation. The soul of man is a part, so to speak, of the *anima mundi*, the soul of the world.

The intellectual soul is a personal manifestation of the "intelligible world" of Plato, the Logos of the New Testament. The spirit is an atom, a monad, an item in the universal spirit. The parts are not scattered fragments, but are inseparably included in the whole, and the whole is in each of the parts. This grand whole, made up of innumerable parts, or the universal world of spiritual intelligence, is called in Sanscrit, Addi-Buddha. In the writings of Paul, it is called the Christ. In it there may be distinct, but never *separate* individualities, any more than there can be separate rays of light.

The spirit has in it the life and power of the sublime unity of spirit. We should never lose sight of this truth. The particular, separate from the universal, is as nothing — it is powerless. The part, sundered from the whole, can do nothing. Even Jesus could say, "the Son can do nothing of himself," or by himself. Echoing this necessary and eternal truth, Emerson says: "The blindness of the intellect begins when it would be something of itself. The weakness of the will begins when the individual would be something of himself."

It was a maxim of the Hermetic philosophy, that "power belongs to him who knows," which refers to the true self, or the spirit. Knowledge is power. But what knowledge will give us the greatest power to save ourselves and help us to save others, and how may we reach the highest consciousness of authority over disease and sin? It is only by climbing up to a position of thought where we can *see* that the self, the immortal *Ego*, is neither diseased nor sinful, but is already saved, and was never lost except to our own consciousness. Its inseparable conjunction with God on this plane of our being makes disease and death an impossible conception to it. Can we gain this loftier altitude of being? Or is it, like the summits of the loftiest mountains, inaccessible to the foot of man? That there is in us a region of being in which divinity dwells, and which is never invaded by evil or sin, or any discomfort, we can easily admit as a theory, but how can we make it real to our consciousness? We can apprehend the idea intellectually; how can we *feel* it to be true? Jesus, as a Son of God, a divinely human spirit, clearly saw and felt this great truth. But the development of sonship in one single person of human history does not fulfil the broadly benevolent design of Christianity. Every one who receives the Logos, the inner divine light and life, becomes also a son of God. (John ii: 12.) That the real self, the spirit of man, and the son of God is exempt from evil and indestructible, is taught in the Jewish and Christian scriptures, and the spiritual philosophy of all antiquity. In the Vedanta it is affirmed, "No weapons will hurt the *self* of man; no fire will burn it; no wind will dry it up. It is not to be hurt. It is imperishable, unchanging, immovable. If you know the *self* of man to be all this, grieve not." If then we are diseased, and sinful, and unhappy, it is not in our true self, and these things are not to be classed among *realities*, but are appearances only. This truth of faith, though dimly seen, like a star from behind a cloud, has in it a redeeming efficiency. For the best remedy for disease and unhappiness is to find out that I am neither sick nor unhappy. This is the knowledge that has in it a saving power. It is a profound truth of Christianity that our true being is included in God, and there is no evil in Him. It was the object of Fichte in his great work, the *Wissenschaftlehre*, or science of knowledge, to search out and discover the first and absolutely fundamental principle of human knowledge. This was supposed to be *unprovable*, for the reason that it was a first principle, and consequently there could be nothing lying back of it that could be a subject of cognition. This first principle must be in itself intuitively *certain*, and must be that which lends certainty to everything else which we know. This absolutely fundamental principle is the *Ego*, or consciousness of self. The *Ego* (the I, the myself), was regarded by him as embracing within itself the whole sphere of *reality*. Outside of it there is absolutely to us nothing. The *Ego* is the subject and the object. It is that which thinks, and that which is thought, the perceiver and the perceived, the feeling and the *felt*. The so-called *non Ego*, or the objects not myself, are known only in myself, and their inmost reality is my thought. This is as far as science can go. It is its *ultima Thule*. But there is a *Beyond*, which Fichte himself entered in after life, as unfolded in his *Destination of Man* and *Way to True Blessedness*. In the region of religious feeling and intuition, and the transcendental realm of *faith*, we rise to the recognition of a still more fundamental principle. It is not merely that *I am*, but this truth arises from another back of it, and out of which it springs,— God *is*, and I am *in* Him, and I am because He is. Our individual self is found, as the Vedanta and Plato, and Jesus and Paul all affirm, to be included in the contents of the Absolute Being or Self.

Outside of this all-comprehending Being, we never can be and be anything. He who feels this, not as an empty, shallow, unenlightened, noisy religious enthusiasm, but is forced to it by a philosophical necessity of thought, will be conscious of a power that partakes of the tranquil omnipotence of God. It is a power which cannot otherwise be attained. It is an immovable fulcrum, more stable than the everlasting hills, on which the lever of faith may rest. Such a person will understand as never before the words of the *risen Jesus*, and the feeling which they express when he affirms that all power in the heavens and the earth was given unto him. (Matt. xxviii : 18.) Having attained to the idea and feeling of oneness with God, being borne up to it by a logical and philosophical necessity, we do not approach disease in ourselves or others, with a curative intention, in our solitary, inflated, but really empty selfhood: but as our individual self *plus* the Godhead, and the whole power and life of nature.

When we act from the external plane of thought and feeling, as we do in our ordinary life in the world, our spiritual and psychological power is at its minimum. When in favored moments, which by habit and culture might become more frequent and prolonged, we retire inward by an introversion of the mind, we climb to a summit of our being where we act as one with God, and all below us in the scale of life is subject more or less to our influence. In proportion as we act from the inmost degree or realm of our existence, we become possessed of a divine and miraculous energy, meaning by a miracle the control of matter by spirit. In harmony with this idea Paul affirms, "I can do all things in Him who strengtheneth me." (Phil. iv: 13.) There is a profound philosophy, or rather theosophy, in this passage. In man and in the wonderful powers of the mind we see the highest exhibition of the Godhead. To say that man is a *part* of God does not express the exact truth, nor the highest verity. He is rather a *manifestation* of God, who is not divisible into fragments or fractions, but is an indissoluble unity and whole. Says Carlyle, who was imbued with the philosophy of Fichte, "To the eye of vulgar logic, what is man? An omniverous biped that wears breeches. To the eye of pure reason what is he? A soul, a spirit, a divine apparition. Well said Chrysostom, with his lips of gold, 'the true Shekinah is man.' Where else is the *God's-Presence* manifested, not to our eyes only, but to our hearts, as in our fellow-man?" (*Sartor Resartus*, pp. 63, 64.)

To act in and from God, and thus possess a power above our ordinary energy, is to attain to a deep conviction that "in Him we live, and are moved, and have our being," in other words it is to feel that our life is included in his Life, and that his Being comprises ours in it. Till we make this discovery, and come to the cognition of this eternal verity, we are weak and spiritually poor. Without it, the angels would no longer "excel in strength." (Ps. ciii : 20.) A man may have a mine of gold hidden beneath the surface of his field, but is none the richer for it until he comes to believe it and know it. Then and then only he attains to a mental appropriation and true possession of it. So we may have in the manifested God, the Christ, the Collective Man, wisdom, and righteousness, and health and blessedness, but if we are blinded by our sensuous mind to this truth, it is all the same as if we had it not. The deepest reality in man is *spirit*, and as a spirit he is an individual, that is, indivisible (as the word means) manifestation of the grand unity of spirit which is God. Even his body, when we take a more penetrating look at it, is a *symbol* of spirit, and not wholly material. It is a complex of spiritual forces, a combination of ideas and sensations, without which it is to us as nothing, and which are wholly included in the life of the soul. There is a region of thought where we translate matter itself into spirit. "Matter," says Carlyle, following the steps of

Fichte, "were it never so despicable, is spirit, the manifestation of spirit; were it never so honorable, can it be more?" (*Sartor Resartus*, p. 65.)

In our spirit, in the inmost centre of our conscious existence, human life, as I have before said, and here again earnestly reaffirm, merges into the Divine. Thence it is that it springs. From that point the stream of life starts, and thence forever proceeds. But this region of the Divine Life in us, and seat of the highest spiritual power, is not an inaccessible solitude that can never be approached and explored by consciousness, as if all access to it were forever closed in this stage of our existence. It sometimes crops out above the surface of our earthly life. It is only the attainment of *the good*, the *to agathon* of the Platonists. In every inspired thought, in each flash of intuition, in every good deed and beneficent act springing from an inward impulse and desire, there is a manifestation of it. The veil of sense is then suddenly rent, in a degree, if not from the bottom to the top, and the holy of holies is laid open to view. The highest attainable state on earth, according to Buddhism, is called *Moksha*, but this is identical with the *eternal life* of the Gospels, and so rendered by Max Müller. This is not unattainable, nor difficult of attainment. Jesus has made the way easy. He who *believeth on the Son* (or Spirit) hath everlasting life. (John iii : 16.) If we had sought it with a hundredth part of the earnestness that men seek wealth, we should long ago have found it. That "eternal life" that was with the Father has been manifested unto us. (1 John i: 2.) We seek it too far off, as something in a foreign land, but it is already in us, and we are in it. We are like a man hunting round the world to find the atmosphere, not realizing, because it is unseen, that it pervades and contains us. When I have discovered myself, I have found *it*. I am it.

To act from a spiritual intelligence, and to be moved by an

unselfish love, is to act from the Divine. He who loveth is born of God, and dwelleth in God, and God in him. (I John iv : 7, 16.) When we approach a patient to cure him of his malady, if we are actuated by a good motive and benevolent intention we are *moved* by him; and if his recovery is agreeable to the divine will, and thus comes within the category of things possible, we are acting in concert with God, and all his power is ours. Our Emerson has well said: "Whilst a man seeks good ends, he is strong by the whole strength of nature. In so far as he roves from these ends, he bereaves himself of power, of auxiliaries; his being shrinks out of all remote channels, he becomes less and less, a mote, a point, until absolute badness is absolute death." (*Nature: Addresses and Lectures*, p. 120.)

I have said that it is a principle of Christianity, and of all spiritual religions, that our true self is included in the being of God. By this I do not refer to the "Unknown," the *Aditi*, pure infinitude, the En-Soph of the Kabala, but to the manifested God, the Christ of Paul. Not the Christ of the popular theology, where the idea shrinks and dwindles down to an isolated personality, but to a larger, fuller, diviner Christ, an eternal, an all-pervading, all-containing, and universal Christ. This is the universal Spirit, the first emanation from the Father, whom no man knoweth, and who is beyond the reach of thought. This Christ is inclusive of all spiritual intelligence, and of all spiritual beings. Neither the Jesus nor the Christ of Paul is a solitary person in the common acceptation of the word, but something more. They are symbols of principles and states that are in us, and in all spirits. This Swedenborg plainly teaches. He says: "That the deepest mysteries lie concealed in the internal sense of the Word, may most manifestly appear from the internal sense of the two names of our Lord, JESUS CHRIST. When these names are pronounced, few have any other idea than that they are proper names, and almost like the names of another man, but more holy; the learned indeed know, that Jesus signifies Saviour, and Christ the Anointed, and hence they conceive some more interior meaning; still this is not what the angels in heaven perceive from these names, their perception extending to things still more divine; for, by Jesus, when the name is pronounced, they understand the divine Good, and by Christ, the divine Truth, and by both the union of good and truth." (*Arcana Celestia*, 3004.)

The word Christ in its etymology is closely related to the Sanscrit *Kris*, the good, the holy, and to the Greek *Chrestos*, the principle of good, identical with Plato's *to agathon*, the Supreme Goodness, who created the world in himself. This idea answers to the Christ of Paul.

The Universal Spirit and all-pervading Divine Presence, and the inmost life of all that is, has, as one of its distinguishing characteristics, inherent in its essence and nature, an irrepressible tendency to *impart*, to extend the sphere of its healing, soul-saving influence. Our proper attitude toward it is one of tranquil desire, passive receptivity, unresisting willingness, and serene trust. The lower soul should be held open toward it, with a suspension of its activity, and by the absorptive power of the soul to imbibe its life. We are not to dictate, but to receive. In the Apocalypse, the living Christ, the only saving, healing principle in the universe, is represented as saying, "Behold, I stand at the door and knock: if any man open the door, I will come in to him." (Rev. iii : 20.) But it is not on the outside door of men's souls that he knocks for admittance, as if he were external to us. The Christ is already within us (Col. i : 27), and he seeks to pass outward into the soul and its body, and permeate these with a higher life. He knocks on the inner door, that opens inward toward God and the kingdom of the heavens; which, if we do not bar against his egress, he will open and pass outward, and become the Saviour (or healer) of the body (Eph. v: 23), and of others through us. In praying to the Christ to save us, we are not merely to *invoke* the Christ or call upon him to come in, but to *evoke* the Christ, who is already in the hidden depths and centre of our being. Even Jesus is *in* the true disciple. (John xvii: 23.) He, as the highest individual expression of the universal Christ-principle, is there as the way, the truth, and the life, and we are to call him forth from the innermost recess of the mind into the outer chamber, and even the external courts of our existence. We look for the Christ as our Saviour, or healer, in the wrong direction, as if he were far off and an absent and distant being, instead of something already in the inmost divine realm of our being. But the righteousness (or right thinking) of faith saith thus: "Say not in thy heart, Who shall ascend into heaven (that is, to bring the Christ down)? or, Who shall descend into the abyss (that is, to bring the Christ up from the dead)? But what saith it? The word is nigh thee, in thy mouth and in thy heart; that is, the word of faith which we proclaim." (Rom. x: 6-8.)

The connection of our inner self with the Supreme Self, and the way in which our spirit is included in the Universal Spirit, or the Christ, may be faintly illustrated by a tree, as, for example, the sacred Banyan, which we will make representative of the Kabalistic "tree of life." In this tree of India, the branches bending to the ground take root and form new stocks, till they cover many hundred feet in circumference. But still it is all one tree, and in the Hindu symbology is called "the tree of knowledge" and "the tree of life," and under its grateful shade the Gurus (instructors) teach their pupils the mysteries of immortality. Every tree is a whole made up of innumerable parts, each of which is a likeness of the whole. I think it was the German poet Goethe who first suggested that the leaf is a typical form, and that every leaf and every bud is, as it were, a tree of itself. This doctrine is now universally adopted in the science of botany. Besides the visible buds and leaves, each of which is an ideal tree, there are a countless number of latent buds that are ready to start into life under the proper conditions. Through each leaf-form the life of the whole circulates, and each leaf when sundered from the tree withers and dies. We as individual spirits sustain the same relation to the Christ. (John xv: 1–8.) We are included in him, and he abides in us. As each leaf is an image and representative of the whole tree, and possesses the qualities and specific virtues of the tree, and as each drop of the ocean has in itself the properties of the great deep, so that if the ocean be salt each drop may predicate saltness of itself, so our true self sustains the same relation to the Christ. If the universal spirit is free from disease and evil, and is always well and tranquilly happy, we may affirm the same of our true self, which is included in it. This is a doctrine of both Jesus and Paul (John xvi: 33; I Cor. 1:30), and also of pre-Vedic Buddhism; and, because of its great practical importance, we shall further discuss it in our next lesson.

CHAPTER V.

HAPPINESS AND HEALTH, AND WHERE THEY ARE TO BE FOUND.

BLESSEDNESS and health are so closely related that they may be viewed as identical and inseparable. Disease has its spiritual counterpart in some mental unhappiness, some inharmony of the inner nature, some spiritual wretchedness, which ultimates itself in the body. For this antecedent mental disturbance we must first find a remedy, or the cure of the body is impossible; or, if it were possible, is of trifling value. To learn how and where to find true happiness, is to discover the best remedy for disease.

To begin our search for this panacea and true *elixir vitæ*, let it be observed that all desirable mental conditions are already in the *spirit* of every man as a possibility; or, as it is expressed in philosophical language, *in potentia*, though they may, for the present, be beyond the region of consciousness or sensation, though they exist as a fact in our inner being, and only wait *recognition*. They may be in a state of latency, like the germ of a plant in the seed, but are capable of being awakened into conscious activity. It has been said of the lotus, the sacred and expressive symbol in the religion of the Hindus and the Egyptians, that its seeds, even before they germinate, contain perfectly formed leaves, and the miniature representation of the perfected plant. This is an instance of præformation or antecedent ideal creation, which has its application to the subject before us. All the happy feelings and emotions that go to make up a state of tranquil blessedness, or spiritual healthfulness, are already in us, and can be aroused from their dormancy or quiescence, and be made to exist *in actu,* or in actual consciousness. Disease on its mental side and in its spiritual essence, as the word itself signifies, is a state of dissatisfaction, an uneasy, disquieted state of the *soul.* Where shall we find relief? Certainly not by looking outward. The true remedy does not lie in that direction. Every one's best teacher, that is *doctor,* is his own inner, divine self, the sage or ancient of days within. Let us ever keep in mind, that all there is or can be in what men call heaven, is already in us, like the miniature plantlet in the seed of the sacred lotus. It is there as a celestial germ. The kingdom of God is within. This narrows down our search for it into a small compass, and heaven is *at hand,* or within our reach. And surely where heaven is, there must be health and happiness. In ordinary language, heaven is represented as above us, and its influences as descending upon us. This is an illusion of the natural or psychical man, a fallacy of the sensuous mind. In the science of correspondence, upward things are interior things. This is a principle as fixed as the laws of geometry. To view God and heaven as above us, is to separate them from us. It is a falsity as great and fatal in religion as it is in mathematics to affirm that the centre of a given circle is external to its circumference. God and heaven are above us only in the sense of being the inmost region of our own being, our inward, divine self. If not here, they can exist for us nowhere. The spiritual man will learn to explore the depths of his inner being in his search for what others vainly seek to find in something external. Happiness, health, and heaven, which in their essence are one, are always within us, and can never by any possibility be external to the mind. To *believe* this, and to know it, is to find them. In the New Jerusalem, which is heaven in man while on earth, or a true spiritual condition developed from within, it is said there is no disease, nor sorrow, nor pain, nor death, "for the first things are passed away"; that is, the sensuous or external action of the mind has ceased to be the governing power, and the man has emerged from the psychical into the spiritual life. From being an animal soul merely, he has become a *spirit*. He has come to himself. He has become a son of man who *is* in heaven. (John iii : 13.) He has risen from the life of sense, which is only an apparent life, and in the New Testament is called death, to the life of the spirit, which is the only real and truly blessed life. Because matter and sense are the greatest barriers between us and the world of pure spirit, it was the aim of the ancient philosophers, from Hermes Trismegistus (the thrice great) down, as it was also of Pythagoras, Gautama the Buddha, and Jesus the Christ, to free the soul of man from the fetters of sense, and its imprisonment in the body, and enable it to begin on earth to realize its Godlike powers. For all of the soul that is in the body is dormant and in a state of lethargy. Its perceptions are illusory and deceptive.

How these higher possibilities of existence and diviner mental conditions, which are inconsistent with disease and cannot coëxist with it, may be evoked from the unconscious region of the mind into conscious activity, is the greatest problem of philosophy and religion. It is a question that outweighs all others in its importance in transcendental science. We will give a few hints towards its solution, just enough to enable every one to place his feet in the *path* and turn his mental eye in the right direction. It shall at least be our office to hold the candle while each one looks for himself.

It is of the first importance, that we learn the truth and never lose sight of it, that as health and heaven are *within* man, so all disturbed and depressing mental conditions are in a region of our being that is relatively external to the *pneuma* or inward divine spirit, which is our real Ego or self. From this external plane of mental action, or of thought and feeling, it is possible for us to retreat inward into a realm of our being where all is peace and unruffled serenity.

> "Distractions are but outward things,
> Thy peace dwells far within.
>
> "These surface troubles come and go,
> Like rufflings of the sea;
> The deeper depth is out of reach
> To all, my God, but thee."

We live too much on the surface of our being and have not even found *ourself*, our real life, which is hid with Christ in God. It is demonstrated by science that there is a depth of the ocean which the most violent storms never stir. Hurricanes that sweep navies from the ocean do not penetrate to this undisturbed realm of nature. This region of placid calmness answers to our true existence, and a poet has so used the correspondence.

> "There's quiet in the deep;
> Above let clouds and tempests rave,
> And earth-born whirlwinds wake the wave;
> Above let fear and grief contend
> With sin and sorrow to the end:
> Here far beneath the tainted foam,
> That frets above our peaceful home,
> We dream in joy and wake in love,
> Nor know the rage that yells above:
> There's quiet in the deep."

So we may turn the mind inward upon itself as far as thought can penetrate; in other words, we can change the direction of the mind from looking outward upon *apparent* things, to a gaze inward, in the direction of our real life and true being, and the mental unhappiness, the pain, the disease of whatever nature it is, will be left without the gate, sundered from our real self. This region of our being is called the secret place of the Most High, the Inscrutable Height of the Kabala, the Divine Internal of Swedenborg, which is the Christ of Paul; and here our truly existing self abides under the shadow of the Almighty, and is the doorway that opens into all the fulness of the Godhead. It is the portico, the piazza, and the anteroom of the sacred temple, our Father's house with many apartments. Here, in finding ourself, we have found God, and, in a deeper quietude than is ever felt in our lower nature, we dwell

> "Too near to God for doubt or fear,
> And share the eternal calm."

It is the region in us where thought becomes a divine force, for the individual spirit consciously abides under the shadow of the Almighty, or the obstructed and tempered light of the divine Truth, adapted to the reception of the finite intellect. The sacred lamp is only shaded by partially transparent glass. It is the region in us of self-control in the fullest sense of the term, and the central throne of the mind's dominion over the body and its diseases. It is the realm of our being where dwells the light of a higher Wisdom, the inward Christ and Son of God, whom Paul found in himself. As one has said, "There is guidance for each of us, and by low listening we shall hear the right word."

> "There syllabled in silence, let me hear
> The still small voice that reached the prophet's ear,
> Read in my heart a still diviner law,
> Than Israel's leader on his tables saw."

In the home of the still small voice, the prayer of faith becomes a saving power issuing from the centre of life. It lies within the compass of our powers thus to retreat inward from disease and our surface troubles, as certainly as it does to fly to our sheltering house from the wintry storm without; and practice will make it easy and repetition a habit.

Things that make us unhappy, and which we call evil, are not so *real* as they seem; but they are shadows that are magnified out of all due proportion. In the Platonic doctrine of creation, the Supreme Goodness is that from which all things proceed, and is that which contains in itself all existing things. This, of course, cannot include anything that is evil. Good is positive and real; evil is the absence of good, and, consequently, has no real existence, only a seeming existence. It is that which is good inverted, or seen with the empty side uppermost. All things, or, as Plato would say, all truly existing things, are from or out of God (I Cor. xi: 12), and what is from Him is and must be good. If then we view disease as an evil, we are forced to the conclusion that it is no-thing. It is emptiness, vacuity, the absence of true being, and has only an apparent existence, a false and fallacious way of thinking which belongs to the lower animal soul. Yet nothing seems more real to the world at large. And so does a shadow to a child, who sees it on the wall, and attempts to pick it off. The sources of our unhappiness are always some false way of thinking. Truth is that which *is*, and falsity expresses what is not. Falsity and non-existence are the same, as when I assert that the angles of a triangle are in their sum either more or less than two right angles, I affirm what has no existence. Now if it can be made to appear that all disease and the sources of our unhappiness are illusions or a false seeming, and hence must count as nothing, it will afford us a secure standing-ground for a saving and healing faith. To assist us in climbing up to this exalted summit of thought will be the object of our next lesson. It is of the first importance that we learn to form the true *idea* of ourselves, and of others whom we would aid into the way of true healing. To form only an intellectual conception of a state, is an incipient creation of it, for certainly the idea is in us, and is a part of us. It may be at first only intellectual; but, between intellect and feeling, as we have before said, there is a law of attraction as between male and female, and the feeling conjoined to the intellectual conception makes it a thing of life, a divine reality. To aid us in this true conception of man, we may look to Jesus, the author and finisher of our faith. (Heb.

xii : 2.) In him, as an incarnation of the universal Christ, we find the point where humanity in general rises into divinity, the point where the highest heavens meet the earth, and blend their higher life and light with our lower plane of existence. If we look to Jesus as the divine model of the true idea of man, we shall find his humanity the needle of a celestial compass that always points due East, toward God and heavenly blessedness. And as representing and including us, we may confidently ask in his name, and receive that our joy may be full. (John xvi : 24.)

There is a region of mental exaltation, or, if you please, of inspiration, where the emptiness and nothingness of what we call evil. and which is the source of our unhappiness, clearly appears. Emerson, who combined in himself both the poet and the philosopher, undoubtedly reached that higher altitude of thought when he wrote : " Good is positive. Evil is merely privative. not absolute ; it is like cold, which is the privation of heat. All evil is so much death or nonentity." Again he says: " I think that only is real which men love and rejoice in ; not what they tolerate, but what they choose ; what they embrace and avow, and not the things which chill, benumb, and terrify them." (*Nature : Addresses and Lectures*, pp. 120, 256.)

This higher altitude of thought, where the evil and the false shrink into nihility, does not appertain to the animal soul, but belongs to that higher range of the mind, that is on a level with the Logos, the spiritual intelligence which is the New Testament faith. We need an Abrahamic faith, before which the visible to sense disappears, and the "invisible appears in sight" to the spirit, and eternal realities are disclosed to the immortal eye, of which the outward organ is the veil. Abraham represents the principle of faith when it rises into intuition, its highest form. He believed in God for what was scientifically and physiologically impossible, and adhered to it with divine obstinacy, until the thing promised became not only a possibility but an actuality. He believed in God who quickeneth the dead, and calleth the things that are not as though they were. (Rom. iv: 17.) We must believe in the same divine principle, which is the Logos or inward Word in us, before which the things that have no existence to the animal soul and sense appear as the only realities. For faith is the *evidence* of things not seen. If it is not this it is only *opinion*.

I CLIMB TO REST.

Still must I climb if I would rest:
The bird soars upward to his nest;
The young leaf on the tree-top high
Cradles itself within the sky.

The streams, that seem to hasten down,
Return in clouds, the hills to crown;
The plant arises from her root
To rock aloft her flower and fruit.

I cannot in the valley stay;
The great horizons stretch away!
The very cliffs that wall me round
Are ladders into higher ground.

To work — to rest — for each a time;
I toil, but I must also climb.
What soul was ever quite at ease
Shut in by earthly boundaries?

I am not glad till I have known
Life that can lift me from my own;
A loftier level must be won,
A mightier strength to lean upon.

And heaven draws near as I ascend;
The breeze invites, the stars befriend,
All things are beckoning to the Best;
I climb to thee, my God, for rest!

(Lucy Larcom.)

CHAPTER VI.

THE REAL AND THE APPARENT IN THOUGHT, OR THE IMPOSSIBLE AND CONTRADICTORY TO SENSE IS TRUE TO THE SPIRIT.

THE source of all real truth is that divine realm of being which we call spirit. But truth in descending (or passing outward) to the plane of the animal soul is inverted. This finds its analogy in the transmission of light through an intermediate lens, as in the camera of the artist, where on the negative plate, which may represent the lower soul, the image is fully inverted, the bottom appearing at the top and the right side on the left. Thus it is in the descent of truth through the three degrees of our being. A glance at our diagram representing the triune constitution of man will make the analogy clearer. This doctrine that our sense-perceptions are an inversion of the real truth, and in spiritual things our senses are never to be believed, is the teaching of Jesus, and Paul, and Plato, and is fundamental in the life of faith. When once established and fixed in our consciousness, it is a truth of momentous practical and saving value.

It was the aim of Jesus to raise his disciples or scholars above the range of the sensuous mind to the perception of real truth. His fundamental precept was of far reaching importance to the man who would attain a truly spiritual life. It was (and still *is*) "Judge not according to appearance (ὄψις, external sight, sense), but judge righteous judgment." (John vii: 24.) This righteous judgment or *rectitude of thinking* is the Kabalistic *justice*, and the Sanscrit *rita*, real truth, and is identical with Paul's "righteousness of faith." For faith is the elevation of the mind above the plane of sense. "We walk by faith, not by *sight*" (ὄψις, appearance, sense) is the maxim of Paul (II Cor. v:7). The words of Jesus above quoted furnish the key to a truly spiritual knowledge. All our sense perceptions are fallacious, and are to be corrected before they are accepted. They never give us the real truth. This was a doctrine of the Hermetic philosophy. On this subject Swedenborg says: "Sensual things, and those which by their means enter immediately into thought are fallacious, and all fallacies which prevail with men are from this source. Hence it happens that few believe the truths of faith, and that the natural man is opposed to the spiritual, that is, the external man to the internal." (*Arcana Celestia*, 5084.) All the profoundest truths, or truths of the spirit, are *contradictions*, that is, they are the direct opposites of the first *appearances*, the *illusions*, the *fallacies* of the *psychical* man. Whatever the natural man, speaking from the plane of sense, affirms, we are to interpret it by opposites, and we get the real truth, just as darkness makes the hidden light of the stars visible, and shows us worlds we never saw by day. In order to aid us to rise from sense to faith, it will be well to demonstrate that all our sense perceptions are an illusion or false seeming. Hence, in judging rightly, they are to be contradicted, and their testimony ruled out.

To begin with, it is a fundamental illusion that we are in time and space, for the direct opposite is true; that is, time and space are in us as modes of thought and feeling, or subjective forms of sensation, as Kant demonstrated. Time is the succession of ideas in our minds, and motion in space is a change of feeling. In common language, when our feelings are stirred we are said to be moved. Hence distance, as it belongs to time and space, is not an external entity, or something outside of us, but is in us as a state of the soul.

THE PRIMITIVE MIND-CURE.

When the scriptures speak of upward things or things above, as God and heaven, mountains and hills, etc., they really mean inward things. To ascend into the hill of the Lord, and stand in the holy place (Ps. xxiv: 3), is to think from the inner realm of consciousness. The Most High is the Divine Inmost in man. The power of the Highest comes upon us when the inmost divine spirit in us is developed into conscious activity (Luke i: 35). To be endued with power from on high (Luke xxiv: 49) has a similar significance. When the primordial point, or Central Life, is placed above us, to go upward is to go inward towards the centre.

All outward things are in *reality* inward things. The objective is the subjective. All the properties of matter are only *sensations* and *ideas* in our minds. The world is not external only as a sensuous seeming, as *Maia* or illusion. It is a mental picture. On this subject, Schopenhauer in "*Die Welt als Wille und Vorstellung,*" says: "The world is my presentation or mental picture — is what I represent it to be; it agrees exactly with my thought; it is my thought. The world exists *for me* only as a picture and a *belief* existent in my mind, only so far as it is portrayed by my thought and present to my consciousness. He prefers, says Prof. Bowen, to call it as Kant did, a Presentation, a Vorstellung, or placing before my mind of certain phenomena or appearances. It is impossible and even inconceivable, that it should be *known* to be anything else than it *appears* to be. Make this mental picture as vivid or life-like as you please, it is still only a mental picture. Whatever the ignorant may fancy, or the superstitious may dream, nothing is known to be behind it. It is only an appearance or presentation. He only is a philosopher, says Schopenhauer, to whom this is distinct and certain. (*Bowen's Modern Philosophy*, p. 394.) All this is true of the human body, which is no part of man, but belongs to the world-picture and is a part of it. If man (or mind) were taken out of the universe, no universe would remain, because there would be no proof, no manifestation, of anything outside of us, when you take away man, that is, mind. For to that alone the world is, and to that alone can it be shown. God created, and still creates, the world through man, says Swedenborg, and we may be allowed to add, only *in* man.

Again. There are no external senses, whatever the psychical, natural, or *soulish* man may believe and affirm, for the simple reason that there is, and can be, no external perception. There are no external sounds, for sound is a sensation, and that exists only in mind. If the music is not in us, it is nowhere. Light and color, which is a modification of light, are not outside of me, but are in me. I am the light. Light belongs only to mind and is a modification of mind. "God is light," says John (I Jno. i: 5), and the converse of this is true, the light is God, or an emanative principle from Him, and is not dependent upon the sun, nor external eyes.

Do we live an individual and independent life? Is my life an isolated fragment sundered from the One Life? Or is it not rather true, as Paul affirms, "In Him we live, and are moved, and have our being"? Then it is no more I that live, but the Christ, the Logos, the inward Word, liveth in me. That is, God only lives, He is the living One, the El Chai. We are taken on board the Universal Life, and can never get outside of it. So God only sees, as Swedenborg sublimely asserts in his comments on Gen. xvi : 13. The external sees from something interior, and this from the inmost, and this last from the Lord. Hence we may say, "Thou God seest me," and I see only in thee, — as was taught in the philosophy of Malebranche, and which was borrowed from the Arabian Al Ghazzali, and he borrowed it from the Hindu metaphysics.

Again, let us ask the natural man, who cannot discern the

things of the spirit, and to whom they are foolishness, Are the senses in our individual soul, or are they not rather included in a universal sense, so that we are in the senses? To be out of this universal sense is to be irrational and insensible. All this will seem to the *psychical* man, as contradictory, and impossible, and is therefore spiritually and sublimely true. There is a universal principle of sense, a *Divine Sensorium*, as Sir Isaac Newton calls it, which is everywhere present, and our individual sense is not disjoined or sundered from it, nor can our senses, as Plotinus affirmed, ever be cut off from it. There is an all-seeing eye, an all-hearing ear, an all-pervading and ubiquitous sense of feeling. True vision is that eye in me, and my hearing is never outside the universal ear or sense. For a true universal is a one thing that is in all things. We must learn to see through the all-seeing eye, and hear through the everywhere-present ear; that is, the Universal Divine Soul, the *anima mundi*. *Then whatever any person in any part of the world sees, or hears, or feels, we may perceive.* This is a great mystery, but is nevertheless demonstrably true. We then have sensation and perception in the universal sense or soul.

Once more, Do we move, or are we really moved? As time and space are in us, as we have shown above, and as all motion must be in time and space, it irresistibly follows, that all motion in its spiritual essence must be in us as a change in our interiors, to use the language of Swedenborg; or, in other words, as a modification of our thoughts and feelings. Hence, motion in its reality is independent of the body. We may be carried away in spirit as Ezekiel was to the river Chebar (Ezek. iii : 14, 15), or like John to an exceeding high mountain (Rev. xxi : 10), and visit any part of the world, and not be missed by our friends in the same room. All this is absolutely impossible, contradictory, and incomprehensible to the psychical man, and hence must be divinely true. It is only what Paul asserts, that " in Him we live, and *are moved*, and have our being." (Acts xvii: 28.) If our life is included in God's life, wherever He is we may and must be. He shares with the spirit of man in a mitigated sense both his omnipresence and omniscience.

Again, it appears to the psychical or *soulish* man that our knowledge is self-originated and is our own. But such a person must become a fool, as the apostle says, in order that he may be wise. (I Cor. iii: 18.) Do we know, or are we known; that is, is our cognition active, or are we passive in knowing? Is not our knowledge *shown* to us? One thing is certain, that we know nothing that is not already known, and which exists in the Universal Mind or Intellect, with which our intellect is conjoined. Paul, one of the profoundest of Christian philosophers, says: "Now we know in part, and we prophesy in part, but when that which is perfect is come (or the true Universal is known, and we grasp the idea of the connection of our mind with it), then that which is in part shall be done away." Then shall we *fully know* even as we also are *fully known* (I Cor. xiii: 9-12), where he expresses the thought, which it is difficult to reproduce in a translation, that all true and perfect knowledge is a passive reception, or that we know all things in and through the Universal Intellect, the Logos or Word, which illuminates every man that cometh into the world. The individual mind is only a mirror, that receives and reflects, but does not shine by its own light. A *passive* knowing is the highest form of intelligence.

It sounds like a contradiction to the natural man, and is, therefore, true to the spiritual mind, that the sense or meaning of the Bible and all good books is not in the letter or the external words, but in us. The book does not in reality enlighten us; but we, as it were, illuminate it. The meaning of words is not in them, but in us. Words are only a sensuous symbol of ideas, and ideas are only in mind, and cannot by any possibility be in Bibles or books. The real Bible is the inward Word, the Logos, the Christ within. In this inward Christ are hid all the treasures of wisdom and knowledge. (Col. ii: 3.) And John says of "young men," which marks a certain stage of spiritual evolution or development, "Ye are strong, and the word of God abideth (or dwelleth) in you." (I John ii: 14.) And if it is not in us, either consciously or unconsciously, it is for us nowhere.

But all this discussion has a practical side to it, and is not mere idle and useless speculation. We have seen that the knowledge (so called) of the *psychical* man or mind, is inverted, and things are seen bottom side up. We must turn them over, and contradict them, in order to come to the perception of the real truth. The knowledge of the sensuous mind is only a false seeming, and is never the real truth, or Paul's righteousness of faith, or rectitude of intellectual judgment. In common language a man says, "*I* am sick," or in suffering or trouble. This is an illusion, as much as when he says the sun rises and sets. His real *self*, his spiritual entity, and immortal *Ego*, is not subject to disease, but this may always affirm, *I am* well and happy. To come to an intuitive perception of this, and hold to it with a divine stubbornness, in spite of the senses, and even reason, is to reach the summit of faith,— a faith that makes us whole. To the sensual man or mind,

> "It would seem
> Less a thing to name or own,
> Than an echo overblown
> From a dream,"

but is nevertheless an eternal reality.

Finally, one of the most impossible and unreasonable conceptions to the psychical or soul-man, and consequently one of the most sublime spiritual truths in the universe is, *that all pain is a positive good and pleasure in the region of our true being.* It is an inner divine good, struggling into a birth in the external range or sensuous plane of our existence. If accepted without opposition, and its outward birth is effected, it ceases as pain, and becomes a pleasure. It is then transmuted into a spiritual delight. The highest spiritual development is born of suffering. When we come to a clear recognition of this, and can view the pain as an interior good, it is instantly alleviated. Here the whole mystery of evil is solved. All evil or pain is an inward, divine, spiritual good, that struggles to ultimate or externalize itself in us, and is opposed and obstructed, consciously or unconsciously, by the soul. But when, by a supreme act of faith, I can bring myself to be willing to suffer, I then cease from suffering, by one of the deepest laws of my being.

If it be true that our spiritual entity is the real man, and son of God, and is, by virtue of its divine and immortal nature, exempt from disease, then the belief of disease is but a *dream*, an illusion, a false seeming. Make it appear to yourself that it is so, and "thou art freed from thine infirmity." Demonstrate this grand truth of faith clearly to a patient, and he is cured. *What men call disease is not disease at all, but only nature's method of curing it.* It is a medicine and not a disease. This is a truth that is capable of an extended illustration.

CHAPTER VII.

DISEASE EXISTS ONLY IN THE MIND ON THE PLANE OF SENSE, WHICH IS THE REGION OF DECEPTIVE APPEARANCES.

It should be our steady aim in all that we do and say, to raise a patient's mind and our own above the mere plane of sense, with its deep-seated illusions. The external body, *with all its diseases*, exists only on that lower range of thought. To elevate the mind above the plane of sense is to exalt our conscious being into the region of faith, where pain and disease cannot exist. This is done to some extent in what is called revery or a waking dream, also in the condition of absent-mindedness, where the mind is withdrawn from external things, and we think in ourselves independent of organic conditions. The first point to be gained is to know our *self;* the next to forget the body and become spirit. The natural or psychical man, or the mind that habitually acts on a level with the body and the senses, sees everything in an inverted order, which is the direct opposite of the real truth. He does not receive (or apprehend) the things of the spirit, nor can he know them, for they are spiritually discerned or judged, as Paul affirms. What men call knowledge, derived from the testimony of the senses, is not knowledge at all, but only error and delusion. When we examine the matter more closely, we are astonished to learn how little we know from sensation. When I say I hear the bell in the church tower, it is not strictly true. All that I hear is a sound which has no meaning in and of itself, but I have learned by association to connect that particular sound with a bell. But if I were hearing it for the first time, it would be impossible for me to know what it was. It is an act of judgment, that is, a decision of the mind on the plane of pure intellect, or what is called in the New Testament and in Plato, faith, which teaches me that a particular sound is connected with a bell, or a coach on the street, or an engine on the railroad. It is one of the offices of faith, or the higher intellect, to interpret the meaning of a sensation. If we have a sensation of discomfort, we can make it signify disease, and this meaning it will bear to us, or we can give it the opposite meaning, and it will bear that signification to us. This is a practical principle. A wrong interpretation of our sensations is a fruitful source of disease.

All that we ever see by the sense of vision, as Berkeley proved long ago, is a sensation of light and its modification in the various colors. Everything else which we attribute to vision is only an act of judgment. Sensation in itself teaches us nothing. As long as the mind is fettered by the senses, true knowledge, which is only another name for faith, is impossible. In disease the senses give us no real knowledge of our true condition. We must learn to disbelieve them, and hearken to the voice of the higher wisdom. Their testimony must be ignored, their fallacies rejected, and the interior mind must assert its divine rights. A true faith, which saves a man body and soul, begins where sensation ends, and is the "evidence of things not seen." In order for faith to become a living power to heal ourselves or others, it must be emancipated from the bondage of the senses. Their clamorous voice must be silenced, and their testimony must be ruled out. This is the true freedom from *matter* that constitutes us spiritual, and essentially and distinctively human. Things look quite different to the mind, when it views them from the spiritual plane of thought and perception from what they do when seen only through the underground window of the dungeon of the prison of sense. To cure ourselves of disease, and remain under the blindness of the senses, is like a shipwrecked mariner trying to keep afloat with a rock attached to him instead of a life-preserver. Disease, having existence only in the mind on the sensuous plane, is so far like all our sense-perceptions a fallacious appearance, and not the *reality* we suppose it to be. The spiritual man will learn to treat it as he does all other illusions. But you will ask me, if the corn on your toe is not as real as the toe itself? To this the answer is, that neither of them have any real existence except as a *thought* on the lower range of the mind, and a false belief; and neither of them is any part of the real Ego or self. Both of them could be removed by surgery and the inner man not be mutilated or touched. Nothing has been subtracted from our true being. When will the world come to the consciousness of the truth, that it is the *pneuma* or spirit, and not the body, that is the man. In its inmost essence it is divine, and, like Milton's angels, immortal in every part. It is never separated from God. The last words of Gautama, when, under the Sâl-tree or sycamore, he was entering into Nirvana, were: "Spirit is the sole, elementary, and primordial unity, and each of its rays is immortal, infinite, and indestructible. Beware of the illusions of matter." The spirit is never separated from God. It is like a wave or ripple on the ocean of being that is never disjoined from the ocean, but is one with it. Or, as the divine Christ in Jesus declares, "I am the vine; ye are the branches, and apart from me, ye can do nothing." (John xv : 4, 5.)

There is a fundamental error which it is important that we correct, for it is the parent of a large class of illusions. I refer to the false belief, the illusive *appearance* of the existence of life and sensation, of pleasure and pain, of health and disease, in the material body. Even motion in its reality or on the spiritual side of it, is not in the body. It is only "a change of state in the interiors," as Swedenborg expresses it. When I raise my arm, the reality of the movement is a modification of the mind. So when we change our position from one part of the room to another, or go from Boston to New York, the real movement is an invisible change in our mental condition. In our dreams we travel through space, and see objects in space and time. But where is that space? It is most certainly *in* us, for by the closing of our senses we are shut off from the outer world. The relation of motion and locomotion to a modification of the mind is a principle that has importance in connection with the subject of vision and action at a distance.

But to return to the subject of sensuous delusions. There is no such thing possible as headache, or what the patient calls the head, for that is never pained. Pain can no more be predicated of the head than of the hat or bonnet. To come to the inward consciousness and certainty of this, is a great step towards the cure of it. Headache in its various forms is only some disturbance, some inharmony or unhappiness in the psychical or soul-principle. But I shall be asked, if the head does not ache, what is it that aches? So the sun appears to rise, but does not. If you ask what it is that rises? the answer is, nothing rises. It is a deceptive appearance, an error that counts for nothing. So of the headache, if the head does not ache, nothing aches. It is an illusion, a false belief of what does not and cannot exist. To intuitively perceive this to be true, is a faith that makes us whole.

The teeth never in reality ache. There has never been such a thing as toothache since the creation of man. The teeth were made for the mastication of food, and it is beyond their function or power to ache. Even Dr. Carpenter, in his *Principles of Human Physiology*, affirms that we do not speak in exact accordance with the truth when we say that we feel a pain in the hand. He would say that it was in the *sensorium*, which is supposed to be located in the brain. But this is a mistake or an illusion as much as the rising and setting of the sun. The brain has no more feeling than the hair, a truth which physiology admits. Dr. Carpenter's affirmation amounts to saying that a feeling exists in what has no feeling. The *sensorium*, or seat of sensation, is not in the body at all, or in any part of it. It is a principle of the transcendental philosophy that time and space are not external entities, but exist in us as modes of thought, time being the succession of ideas in the mind, and space the *distinguishing* of things, or the viewing of them as distinct rather than all at once. But as both time and space are in us *as modes of thought*, it follows that *we locate a pain by thought and in thought*. But we have the same power to deny its existence in any particular part of the body, or to locate it outside of the body, that we have to think at all. The phenomenon of misplaced sensation is one familiar to physicians and physiologists. Where we *think* a pain to be, there it is to us, for it exists only in thought. To put it out of thought is to annihilate it. The same is true of disease in the proper sense of the word. By thought and in thought we give it locality. But if it is not in the body, which is intuitively true, and not in the spirit, which is the real self, then where is it, you will ask? It exists in the animal soul as a false way of *thinking*. It may come to us from the general current of the world's life, an established wrong belief in the collective soul from which we are not disconnected. It is the office of faith to correct this established "public opinion," and lift us out of its disordered current. Faith disowns the disease or discomfort as belonging to the *non-ego*, or the " not me," and by doing this we free ourselves from it and relegate it to its source.

With regard to other diseases, we may affirm that paralysis is not in the body. It is a loss of *desire* and *will*, which are the spiritual principle of motion. Nervous diseases, as they are popularly called, are not in the nerves. This popular notion or current *opinion* which is encouraged by the learned ignorance of the various schools of medicine is only superficial nonsense. The nerves are innocent of any fault. General debility is not a physical condition. Weakness and strength cannot in strict propriety be predicated of the bodily organism, as the five hundred muscles are not a force any more than an engine is a force. In the latter the expansive power of steam is the energy that moves the powerless machinery, and even this has its seat in the universal world-soul or life-principle. General debility, for which we give Peruvian bark and iron, is a mental languor. Every one knows how a little pleasurable mental excitement increases the strength and invigorates the whole muscular system. Nausea is not in the membranes of the stomach, but is either a conscious or unconscious feeling of repugnance and antipathy in the soul. The very *thought* of a disgusting object causes us to express it by a movement as if we were about to vomit. Is it then the object or the thought of it that makes us sick? But you will ask, "Is poison in the material substance or is it in us?" If I affirm it is not necessarily in the drug, you will kindly ask me to swallow stricnia or Prussic acid. You will excuse me if I answer you in the language of another under analogous circumstances: "Get thee behind me, Satan, for it is written, Thou shalt not tempt the Lord thy God." The truth seems to be that in the spiritual or immaterial essence of Prussic acid there is something antagonistic to the life-principle in us. It is certainly given in medicine *in small quantities*, so that below a certain amount it is not considered deleterious, but useful. Then it is not the thing itself that kills, but the quantity. What we affirm, and which is the only practical principle in relation to the subject is, that having swallowed it accidentally, so that we have not by our presumption "tempted the Lord our God," there is a power in a true faith (if we have it or can get it) that will *save* us from its effects. The lower law of its deadly influence will be suspended by the action of the higher law of faith. For this we have the authority of Jesus the Christ. (Mark xvi: 17, 18.) If a person swallows only a small amount of stricnia, but under the *impression* that it is a large quantity, it will intensify its effects. If, on the other hand, we swallow an overdose, but believing and thinking it only a *small* quantity, it will mitigate its influence. If our mode of thinking in regard to it thus affects its action, why is it unreasonable that faith may wholly repeal the natural law of its action? And if it is thus an antidote to poison, and annuls the law of its action, why may it not cure all diseases that are curable? Perhaps our best remedy is found in the simple prayer, "Lord, increase our faith."

We might continue this discussion in regard to the mental aspect of disease, and the common illusions respecting it, and affirm that dyspepsia is not a condition of the stomach, and so on through the whole catalogue of ills that flesh is supposed to be heir to. But enough has been said to illustrate a general principle. The whole practice of materialistic medication will seem to the spiritual man as absurd as it would be to take the invalid and place him in the sunlight, and then apply the remedies to the shadow of the man rather than to the man himself. In the system of Jesus, the body was healed by saving and restoring the soul. So, in the employment of spiritual forces and metaphysical agencies in the cure of an invalid, we ignore the body so far as to view it only as the *umbra* of the real man, and direct our attention to the morbid *idea*, the mental image of the disease in the mind of the patient. The importance of this procedure we shall endeavor to show in our next lesson. We do this on the self-evident principle that an effect will disappear on the removal of its cause, as an effect exists in its cause, and is one with it. They must both stand or fall together. We act also on the principle laid down by Jesus, that "it is the spirit that maketh alive; the flesh profiteth nothing." (John vi: 63.) To direct our attention, as is usually done, to the body only, is to aim away from the central mark, and of necessity to miss it.

CHAPTER VIII.

THE DEEPEST REALITY OF DISEASE IS A MORBID IDEA AND BELIEF.

IDEAS, as we have before shown, are conceptions, or the union of thought and feeling on the intermediate plane of our being. By a morbid idea we mean a false or erroneous intellectual way of thinking, which, if it becomes a fixed mode of thought, is united to the correlative feeling. This is the inner history of the genesis of all disease. Every material thing in the universe, including the so-called physical diseases, exists in us as an idea, without which it has and can have no existence for us. For the idea of a thing and the thing itself, are not two separate and distinct entities, capable of an existence independent of each other, but together they constitute an inseparable and indivisible unity. Remove the idea of a thing, as of a chair, a table, or a coin, or of a so-called bodily malady, as is frequently done in the magnetic state, and from a law of necessity, the thing or object disappears. The substance being removed, the phenomenon, the appearance, the shadow, goes with it. The properties or sensible qualities of all the objects of nature, as Berkeley unanswerably demonstrated, cannot exist independent of or outside of a percipient mind. They exist in our minds as thoughts and ideas, and as a feeling which we denominate a sensation. If we remove from our minds, or from the mind of a patient, the mental image or idea of the malady, the disease will vanish as certainly as to remove an object from before a mirror will cause the disappearance of its reflected image. In proportion as the idea and the *belief* of a malady are effaced, it will weaken its grasp upon us. Here is the direction in which we should perseveringly aim, whatever therapeutic devices we may employ. In certain cases, and under the proper conditions, it may be done instantaneously, but is more frequently effected gradually. A foggy atmosphere does not clear away at once, like the rolling up of the curtain in a theatre, but it slowly lifts to show us "the whitely shining hills of day." The sun in rising does not shoot up like a rocket from a vessel in distress, but the daybreak grows into the full morning.

When I affirm that to remove from the mind of an invalid the idea of a disease, will cause the disappearance of his malady, I feel myself standing on an established philosophical ground, an impregnable scientific position. In order to dislodge me from it, it must be shown that a person can have a pain, or discomfort, or any unhappiness, and not perceive it or know it. But the problem for a true medical philosophy to solve, is how to effect this radical change in the mental *status* of the patient. How can we revolutionize his mode of thinking, and pluck from his mind the deeply-rooted idea of disease? Knowledge is power, and truth is omnipotent. That which is seemingly impossible is easily done if we know how to do it. Truth is the kingly principle. Say the Hindu sacred books, "Royal rule is in its essence truth. On truth the world is based. Truth is lord in the world. All things are founded on truth, and there is nothing higher than it."

We know it as a fact that has often come under our observation, that the dislodging from the mind of a patient of a morbid idea, with its accompanying *fear and unbelief*, which has come to have a controlling influence, and the substitution in its place of the opposite idea and belief, has often effected an immediate and radical change in his physical condition. Let us take an illustrative case, for which nearly every one's memory will be able to furnish a fact parallel with it. During the prevalence of an epidemic fever, a person affected with a slight cold, or any combination of disagreeable sensations, forms the *idea* that he is seized with the malady in its incipient stage. While this belief reigns undisturbed, he is, and will continue to be, sick of a fever. Under the dominating influence of this idea, he suspends his business and takes to his bed. At this juncture of affairs, the family physician, in whose skill and judgment he implicitly *relies* arrives on the scene. He is one of an ever-growing number, who is rising from the lower dignity of a physician, a dispenser of drugs, to the higher office of a *doctor* or teacher. On a careful and searching diagnosis of the case, he assures the patient that his anxiety is groundless, his fears without foundation; that he is laboring under an *error*, and that the dreaded malady is not a fixed actuality. This view of the case is accepted, and supplants and dethrones the other, and in a brief time, as if a mill-stone had been lifted from his condition, the man rises from disease to health, and to the active discharge of the duties of his calling.

It is to be remarked that fear as a form of unbelief, or rather *misbelief*, and which is the tap-root of many a disease, is but a suppression of faith, and not an extinction of the power or faculty of believing. Hence, when fear is removed, faith, its opposite, naturally and spontaneously arises. The allaying of the fears of a patient is equivalent to the excitation of a saving or healing faith. Just as when a spiral spring is pressed down by a superincumbent weight, if that is removed, the spring returns by its own elasticity to its proper position. So if by the divine power of truth, we can lift from an invalid that which really holds him down, he will " arise, take up his bed, and walk."

Let us return to the supposed case we have before us. Hundreds of facts might be given which in principle are identical with it, and in all essential particulars are only repetitions of it. Let us carefully scrutinize the mental principles involved in the cure. There was a *desire* to get well, for we take it for granted that the man was not a professional invalid. This desire included in it a *willingness* to use the proper remedy. There was a *confidence* in the knowledge and skill of the physician, and this was sufficiently strong as of necessity to constitute a pre-disposition and tendency to *believe* his suggestions, and to adopt his ideas and way of thinking. There was also a ready *submission of the will* to the directions of the physician and *faith* in their efficacy. In this condition of mind, the kindly positive and authoritative affirmations of the physician changed the mode of the patient's *thinking* in regard to his disease. The idea of the fever was at once weakened, and obscured, and finally blotted out of the mind, and, with its disappearance, the disease vanished. It was like meeting a man descending a mountain road which we are ascending. We face him directly round in the opposite direction, take him by the hand and lead him calmly up toward the summit, with its view of the promised land. This case, carefully studied, will be found to contain, compressed into a small compass, the arcane spiritual philosophy of every cure effected by any of the prevailing methods, and especially of the marvels of healing wrought by the Christ. And by putting ourselves into the same attitude toward Him to-day as the patient was supposed to have done toward his physician, *He will heal us to-day in both soul and body.* "He that cometh unto me I will in no wise cast out" has never yet been proven false. If it does in your case, it will be the first in the history of the world.

How and by what means this change is to be wrought in the mental *status* of an invalid is a matter to be decided by the skill and judgment of the physician. There is no way in which it can be done without his consent and coöperation. Wilt thou be made whole, or wish you to get well? must be answered in the affirmative, verbally or silently. We can lift a man from the water, while drowning, by main strength and in spite of himself. But disease is not cured in that way. We shall have to accommodate ourselves to the different stage of mental and spiritual development in which men are found. We must sometimes descend towards the level of their platform in order to raise them to ours. We must condescend to their position, and come into a certain sympathy with them in order to take them back with us to our higher view. This principle of sympathy is supposed by the Hindu Mozoomdar to furnish the key to the mystery of the cures effected by the Christ. But it is not sympathy with the disease, but sympathy with the true *idea* of the man which is obscured by the disease. By coming into sympathy with this, the two become stronger than one.

When we attribute the generation of diseased conditions of the body to some antecedent abnormality of mind, we do not mean to teach that a given disease, as rheumatism, or dyspepsia, is the instantaneous creation of a sudden thought, or the unexpected advent of an idea to our consciousness. The disease may be the fixed ultimation, or translation into a bodily expression of modes of thought and feeling long anterior to our first recognition of it. A person will say: "I was sick before I thought anything about it; as, for instance, I woke up in the night with a severe cold." This means in reality that you woke up *thinking* that you had caught a cold, or more properly that the cold had caught you. To say that you had a cold without thinking about it, is in reality affirming that you had a cold without *knowing* it; for you certainly never knew it until you thought of it. Hence you are testifying to what you do not know, and, consequently, as a witness in this case, you are ruled out. You mean in what you say, that you awoke in the night and became conscious of certain unpleasant sensations, which were interpreted to mean a cold. But faith could have given a different meaning to them, and you would have escaped the cold. Or, if you had never thought anything about it, you would have remained until this day in blissful ignorance that you had ever had a cold.

The true spiritual physician will never forget, whatever the temptation may be to do so, that there is a higher therapeutic efficiency in an *idea* than in any drug known to medical science. In the language of the learned German professor, Johannes Müller, "The influence of ideas upon the body gives rise to a great variety of phenomena, which border on the marvellous." He illustrates this by a case mentioned by Pictet. A young lady who wished to experience the intoxicating effects of the nitrous oxide gas, which she had at different times before inhaled, came to Pictet for that purpose. But, in order to test the power of the imagination, common atmospheric air was given to her. She had scarcely taken two or three inspirations of it, when she became insensible and exhibited all the effects of the nitrous oxide. The question arises, what was it that so affected her? Was it anything more than an idea, and a *belief?* Surely then the influence attributed by Jesus to simple faith is not unreasonable, though its saving power is discounted in these days of gross material medication. The influence of ideas, Müller asserts, when they are combined with a state of emotion, generally extends in all directions, affecting the senses, motions, and secretions. But even simple ideas, unattended by any excited state of the feelings, produce most marked effects upon the body. (Müller's *Elements of Physiology*, Vol. II., p. 1392.) This is an important testimony from a high authority.

Müller lays down the general law that an idea having reference to a secretion (and the same is true of any physiological action) causes a stream of nervous energy to be directed towards the secreting organ, and if the mind is at the same time influenced by an emotion, the effect just mentioned is more marked. But what Müller denominates the nervous energy I prefer to call the universal, divine life-principle in nature, the *akasa* (pronounced a*h*asa) of the Hindu metaphysics, an all-pervading, omnipresent, vivific principle of life and motion identical in its higher aspects with the Holy Spirit of the Gospels. An act of faith determines a current, so to speak, of this inconceivably subtle life-force toward the result aimed at and desired. Hence through faith, which is but a mode of thought in union with feeling, a disease is curable that otherwise would be incurable.

It is a peculiarity of the Hindu mind that it is transcendental, and gives more reality to the supersensuous, and especially to thought, than is done in our European and American philosophy. The subjective and objective become one. In the Lânka Vâtara, one of the sacred books of Buddhism, it is said: "What seems external exists not at all, only the soul manifests itself in different forms." Again it is affirmed, "All worlds are but the creation of our thought." This sounds like the words of Fichte in his algebraic formula, "*the Ego equals the non-Ego*," or external things are included in the Ego or inner self. Even Condillac, who reproduced the sensational philosophy of Locke in France, though a materialist, was compelled to say, "Though we should soar into the heavens, though we should sink into the abyss, we never go out of ourselves; it is always our own thought that we perceive." Neither Berkeley, nor Fichte, nor Schopenhauer ever said more than this. The doctrine taught by Buddhism twenty-five centuries ago has come down through Christianity, and is faintly heard as a dying echo in Emerson; so faint that few even hear it at all. He says, "All that you call the world is the shadow of that substance which you are, the perpetual creation of the powers of thought, of those that are dependent, and those that are independent of your will." (*Nature: Addresses and Lectures*, p. 324.)

Our doctrine is nothing new, and need not be startling

We are intensely conservative, as was Jesus the Christ, who says no man who has drunk old wine, or tasted the ancient spiritual truth, straightway desires the new, for the old is better. This is not common bar-room talk about the quality of wines, but has a deeper meaning. And you will allow me to say, that in the Gospels and the Epistles of Paul, there is a rich and fertile stratum of sub-soil that the common religious plow does not turn up. The surface of the vineyard is becoming exhausted, and unless we plough deeper we shall raise but a meagre crop.

That the doctrine of this lesson is not new, but belongs to an old philosophy and archaic wisdom-religion, I present as a proof but one more quotation. In the Dhammapada, one of the books of the sacred Canon of Buddhism, among the brief religious sentences of which it is made up we find these golden words: "All that we are is the result of what we have thought; it is founded on our thoughts, it is made up of our thoughts."

Five hundred years before Sakya Muni, Solomon says: "As a man thinketh in his heart, so is he." (Prov. xxiii : 7.) A thousand years after Solomon, under the modifying and exalting touch of the higher wisdom in Jesus, it becomes the central principle in his scheme of human redemption, "Be it unto thee according to thy faith." (Matt. ix : 29.)

CHAPTER IX.

THE SCIENCE OF OBLIVESCENCE, OR THE ART OF FORGETTING A MALADY.

THE possession of a good memory, that holds all truth in its capacious grasp ready for use whenever an occasion arises which calls for it, is one of the most valuable of our mental attainments. But there are times, and especially in disease and in our transient and permanent states of unhappiness, when we could be tempted to exchange it for the ability to forget, the power to change the direction of our thoughts, and expunge from the tablet of our minds the morbid ideas that will not depart at our bidding. Like a lingering and unwelcome visitor we bid them adieu and hope we are rid of them, but they come back again through the unbolted door. They are birds of evil omen, that not only fly unbidden over our heads, but build their nest in our outhouse, and will not be scared away. In the cure of a man's disease (or in the healing of ourselves), we are to attend to these false and fallacious ideas. Here is the seat of the trouble, and where the remedy is to be applied. In showing that disease exists on its spiritual and real side as a morbid idea, we have driven the animal to his lair, and can now suspend the chase and raise the question of the best method of extermination. A new idea, when it is so administered to an invalid as to be appropriated and to become a fixed mode of thinking, and is not hastily thrown off by a mental excretion, renews the entire man, soul and body. Since thought and existence are one and the same, if we change a man's mode of thinking and believing, we modify his whole life, as certainly as an alteration in the direction of the wind from west to east will cause the vane on the church-spire to point eastward. But to dislodge from the mind of a patient a morbid idea, that has become fixed and maintains its hold with an obstinate steadfastness, is the most difficult work the intelligent medical practitioner has to perform, and one that few ever undertake to do, hence "They heal the hurt of the daughter of my people slightly," or in part only (Jer. viii: 11). To do this requires more skill than to amputate a limb or select the right drug. The common medical practice is like coming to the rescue of a man who has fallen among robbers; we secure his valuables, but leave the man in the hand of his enemies. To change the way of a patient's thinking, or even our own, might at first seem as much an impossibility as to change the skin of the Ethiopian, or the spots of the leopard. It is not enough to paint the skin of the one, or dye the hair of the other. This is superficial. After the return of Berkeley from a journey in France, he was stricken down with a fever. On his recovery, his friend, Dr. Arbuthnot, wrote to Dean Swift, "Poor philosopher Berkeley has now the *idea* of health, which was very hard to produce in him; for he had an *idea* of a strange fever upon him so strong that it was very hard to destroy it by introducing the contrary one." What the learned and justly celebrated physician meant for a good natured witticism, contains a profounder philosophy of human nature than the medical schools ever teach. We have before shown that the idea of a thing and the thing itself are not two distinct and separate entities, but are an indivisible unity and unbroken whole. The idea, as the German idealists maintain, is the *ding an sich*, the thing in itself; the object is the phenomenon, the appearance, the shadowy representation of it; or, as Swedenborg, following the terminology of the Schoolmen, would say, the one is the *esse*, the other the *existere* derived from it. This he always affirms is the relation of the soul and its body. (*Heavenly Secrets*, 10,823.)

What we must aim at in the treatment of a given malady is permanently to efface the idea and belief of it. If things have existence to us only as we think of them, then to put them out of thought is practically to annihilate them, as we have shown in a previous volume. There are works on the art of memory with directions how to improve the retentive power of that faculty, and these volumes have their value in the education of the young. But what an invalid, who remembers too well and too much, most needs to learn is the art of forgetfulness, the blessed science of oblivescence. We are told in all works on mental philosophy, that we best and longest remember that on which we often and intently fix the attention. So, on the other hand, in proportion as we cease to attend to anything, or to fix the thoughts upon it, the idea fades from the mind and ceases to be to us an actuality.

It is oftentimes amusing, as well as marvellous, to see what an invalid can do when, for some reason, he *forgets* his disease. The coming into mind of some more influential thought, so that the idea of disease drops out of consciousness, will effect in reality as great results as those about which we read in the advertisements of patent medicines. We were knowing to a case of rheumatic lameness of long standing where the patient, under the diverting influence of an absorbing conversation, was seen to walk for a fourth of a mile without any show of lameness. At length he paused short in the road and exclaimed that he had forgotten to limp! and, as it was so late in the journey, he concluded not to begin. An older brother of ours, who was disabled by the severing of the large ligaments of the right ankle, in his wakeful hours could not step his foot on the floor; yet in a state of somnambulism would go where it would seem wellnigh impossible for a person in full wakefulness and soundness of limb to transport himself. In the somnambulic state he forgot both his lameness and his body. The inner and real man walked and climbed, and the passive body accompanied it. The wife of a tailor in New Hampshire, who had been confined to the bed for years as a helpless and hopeless invalid, was awakened in the middle of the night by the flames in her room. The house was on fire, and there was no time for debating the question whether she could rise and walk or could not walk. The all-absorbing thought of the impending danger effaced from her mind the idea of disease, and this suddenly dropped out of consciousness, and in spirit she ran out of doors, and the body went with it. In her case the cure was permanent. These cases were not miracles, but facts in harmony with law — the sovereignty of the mind over the body. The time is not in a very remote future when people will be educated in the use of these latent and now dormant, because unused, psychological powers. In a speech, made many years ago in the city of New York by Kossuth, he says that when governor of Hungary, he was at times nailed to his bed by sickness (to use his own expression), but news would come from the army that demanded all the strength of his activity, and in the exercise of that self-originating power of thought that is usually but erroneously called free will, he would say to his body, "Be well," and it obeyed him. This was not merely the command of a despotic will, issuing its ukase to the body, which is as useless as to issue an order to a rock to fly, but it was an act of *faith* — the same faith which has subdued kingdoms, wrought righteousness, obtained promises, stopped the mouths of lions, quenched the violence of fire, escaped the edge of the sword, and to sum up its sublime effects in a few words crowded with meaning, *out of weakness has made men strong.* (Heb. xi : 33, 34.) If faith as a causal agent and power will accomplish such results, is the cure of disease by it to be deemed an incredible and impossible achievement?

But the oft-repeated question will again arise in the reader's mind, "How am I to get this faith?" The very question involves in it a fundamental mistake. You are not to get it in any way, but to *use* it. We are looking for what we already possess, like a man who is asked to lift an obstruction out of his path, and he inquires, "Where are my arms with which I can do it?" Faith is only the action of the mind above the plane of sense, with its false and deceptive appearances. In the atmosphere of the world of both matter and mind, there is a lower and an upper stratum that move in opposite directions. Like an adventurous aeronaut, we must cut the cable of sense that holds us to the earth and its illusions, and we shall rise into a current of thought that will bear us in the opposite direction, away from the West toward the East, the true orient, the home of the rising sun, the origin of things. In the cases mentioned above, the *inner man* broke through the chrysalis encasement of the senses, and seized the helm and turned the vessel, about to founder in a storm, in the opposite direction. To discover the inward and supreme man, the true self, is to come into the possession of faith. He is invisible and concealed behind a thin curtain, and by a signal can be summoned to our aid. The Being whom we call God is the most intimately present and active force in the world, but is deeply veiled from sight.

It must be kept in mind that all causes are absolutely invisible to the external senses. They exist in a realm of being of which the senses are not and cannot be cognizant. It is only effects that are ever discernable to the sensuous degree of the mind or the psychical man. When I exert a certain mental energy, which we name volition, I raise my arm. The visible motion is but the outward expression of an unseen mental force. So when I move a chair or a table, the *power* which does it is out of sight. Take as an illustration the apparent movement of one ball by another on a billiard table. The first ball is not the *cause* of the motion of the second, but the real cause lies further back. It originates in the mind of the player. He makes an exertion of will which communicates a motion to the muscles of his arm. This is transmitted to the cue that is held in his hand, and through this it is communicated to the first ball, through that to the second, and so on. But the only cause is a mental force or act which is an invisible spiritual energy. In a way analogous to this God governs the world, and we our bodily organism. We must fix it in our thought as a fundamental axiom that matter in all its modifications, forms, movements, conditions, and qualities, whether in the human body or the world at large, is never anything but an effect, of which some spiritual force is the originating and governing cause. The absolute impossibility and non-existence of physical causation is a prominent article in the creed of the spiritual man. The body can never affect the mind. But turn this affirmation bottom side up and you get the truth. But it is said that if you tie a ligature around the arm or the leg, it will interfere with the circulation and obstruct the healthy action of the limb. This is admitted, but before we surrender our position we may be allowed to pause and inquire if the cord tied itself, or was it somebody's *mind and will* that tied it? Does a billiard ball or a boy's marble ever move itself? It does just as much as the world or the human body ever moves itself. Now the principle of all motion and the realm of causation belong to the "unseen" but real world. And when we are in the *interior state*, and act from that region of our being, we are in the realm of causation, and the thoughts and volitions of the spirit become themselves causes, especially when they act in harmony with the benevolent aims of the Universal Mind, of which our minds are only personal limitations.

We know that one mind can affect another mind, and thus affect the body. This is a demonstrated fact, as much so as any principle of Chemistry. Says Dr. George Wyld, "The very common experiment of blindfolding certain individuals and then touching them with one finger, or sometimes willing them without contact, and thus influencing them to act according to your *secret thoughts* demonstrates the silent action of mind on mind, and through this on the bodies of other persons." (*Theosophy and the Higher Life*, p. 27.) I simply recommend this power of the mind, as I have done for twenty-five years, in the cure of disease in ourselves and others. It can be made to inaugurate and accelerate an impulse towards recovery. Do not the above-mentioned interesting psychological phenomena render its use for that purpose rational and worthy of trial?

The phenomena mentioned by Dr. Wyld may seem trifling and frivolous. So does the movement of the marbles by a boy in his sports, yet he employs a force like that by which God moves the worlds in their orbits. To raise our curative effort above the appearance of trifling, our silent suggestion may take the form of unspoken prayer, that summons to our aid the Central Power of the universe. We shall illustrate this principle of silent suggestion more fully in our next lesson.

It only remains in the language of Paul to answer the question, "How may we get faith?" Says the inspired apostle, "Faith cometh by hearing, and hearing by the word of God." (Rom. x:17.) The original term for hearing (*akoe*) means instruction in a derivative sense, the listening or hearkening to a teacher. But the teacher is the Word of God, not a book, but a *rema*, a flowing out, an emanation from God. The same word is used by Jesus when he affirms that man does not live by bread alone; in fact, not at all, but by an emanative life and light from God. (Matt. iv:4.) This principle of light and life, this true bread of life, is that primal emanation from God which we name the Universal Spirit, of which our spirit is an individualized expression.

"The spirit of man," said Solomon, "is the candle of the Lord, searching all his inwards parts." (Prov. xx: 27.) Now a candle does not in reality shine by its own light, but is a manifestation of a universal luminiferous principle of light. So the spirit of man is a finite limitation of the Universal Spirit, the Christ of Paul, and the true light of every man that cometh into the world. In our worldliness we have covered it with a bushel, an opaque veil of sense. But the precept of the higher wisdom in Jesus is, "*Let* your light shine." (Matt. v: 16.) It is in a perpetual endeavor, as all light is, to shine, but we prevent it by our impenetrable and commercial bushel. We limit and measure it as the merchant does his produce kept on sale. We are enjoined to *let* our light shine. We are not to institute a long series of efforts and devices to *make* it shine. We are not to blow "the candle of the Lord" as a man would the smoking embers of his fire, for by that procedure we are in danger of blowing it out. But remove the bushel and assume an attitude of listening, which a true disciple always takes, and like the one in Patmos, we shall turn to *see* the voice that speaks (Rev. i: 12), for it is that inaudible word or emanative light of truth which proceeds from the mouth of God.

> "Hearken, hearken!
> Shall we hear the lapsing river
> And our brother's sighing ever,
> And not the voice of God?"

CHAPTER X.

THE INCIPIENT IDEA OF RECOVERY, AND WHENCE DOES IT COME?

THE first indication of recovery from disease is discernible in the consciousness of the patient in the *idea*, the *impression*, the *belief* however faint, that he is recovering and will ultimately get well. This prophetic idea is the initial step up the ladder on which we climb from disease to health. It does not in reality, but only in appearance, follow any favorable bodily change. It is the herald of the subsequent recuperation of the physical powers. It is anterior to any favorable modification of the bodily symptoms, the John the Baptist in the wilderness of our disordered condition, announcing the approach of the kingdom of God in us. It is not an effect of an antecedent physical change, but a cause. The spiritual idea is the forerunner bearing the news of the coming victory of spirit over matter; and if the idea is accepted and finds lodgement in the consciousness, it silently and with divine celerity goes to work to adjust the body into its outward expression, or to translate the language of heaven into the vernacular of sense. It is the secret Logos, the creative Word, the invisible divine force that in all creation works from within outward.

But whence comes this sanative idea, this creative thought, this healing belief? It certainly comes from the universal realm of mind, and issues from the spiritual world of which our minds are a part, for all ideas belong to that boundless realm of life. As that world is in a perpetual endeavor, and has in its nature a conatus to impart good and truth to us, as certainly as the all-surrounding atmosphere is by its pressure striving to fill every vacuum, the patient may receive it directly from the Universal Mind, if his soul is held passively open and upward to imbibe and absorb its influx. We know that to whisper in a person's ear will wake him out of sleep, if not as quickly, still as certainly, as to blow a trumpet. So the Logos, the Metatron, or redeeming angel of the Jewish Kabala, the inward voice, whispers in our inner ear to arouse us from the lethargy of the life of sense to the life of the spirit. Even Jesus may thus speak to the true disciple if the inner ear is attuned in harmony with celestial music, and the sheep may still hear the voice of the good shepherd. It is not the Christ who has become dumb; we are only hard of hearing. If we turn the inner ear towards the ever-present Universal Christ, we shall " hear the heart of silence throb with a soundless word," as the mystics of all ages and all lands have done. The secret Logos, the true light of life, is concealed in the depths of our own being. It speaks to men in the advent of a saving idea clothed in silence,— a deep and calm revealing. This is not a new doctrine, but a former friend and acquaintance, who has been so long absent from this materialistic generation, that we have forgotten his countenance. It is not a doctrine that belongs to a shallow, religious enthusiasm, but to philosophy as well; from the Hindu Upanishads down through Sokrates, with his *daimonion*, or inward divine voice, into Christianity, where in the church it has wellnigh been buried out of sight. On this subject the Rev. John Norris, who reproduced in England the philosophy of Malebranche, when writing about 1690, says that " the Divine *Nous*, or Eternal Wisdom, is intrinsically with or præsential to the mind, and we see and understand all things in Him. From this it necessarily follows that the right and only method of inquiry after that truth which is perfective, is to consult the Divine Nous or Eternal Wisdom. For this is the region of truth, and here are hid all the treasures of wisdom and knowledge. It is that great and universal oracle lodged in every man's breast, whereof the ancient Urim and Thummim (lights and perfections) were an expressive type and symbol. This is reason; this is conscience; this is truth; this is that light within, so darkly talked of by some who have by their awkward, untoward, and unskilful way of representing it, discredited one of the noblest theories in the world. But the thing in itself, rightly understood, is true; and if any man shall yet call it Quakerism or enthusiasm, I shall only make this reply at present, that it is such Quakerism as makes a good part of John's Gospel and Augustine's works. But to return: this, I say, is that *Divine Oracle* which we all may and must consult, if we would enrich our minds with truth — that truth which is perfective of the understanding. And this is the method of being truly wise. And this method is no other than what is advised us by the Divine Nous, the substantial Wisdom of God (Prov. viii: 34): "Blessed is the man that heareth me, watching daily at my gates, waiting at the posts of my doors." And again, says the same substantial Wisdom: "Whoso is simple (sincere, honest) let him turn in hither." (Prov. ix: 4.) And again, "I am the light of the world; he that followeth me (or as the word more properly signifies, ho that consorts or keeps company with me), walketh not in darkness, but shall have the light of life." (John viii: 12.)

This, therefore, is the *via intelligentiæ*, the way and method of true knowledge, — to apply ourselves to the Divine *Nous*, the eternal Wisdom of God. But this is to be found only in that region of our being which is in accord with it, and an inlet to it.

The initial idea of recovery may come to the patient through the influence of others; for how much our silent fears and forebodings on the one hand, and our hopes and our faith on the other hand, may have to do with the varying condition of the sick, we do not fully realize. A disabled and leaky vessel may be saved from going down and brought safely into port by attaching it to a strong and well-built steamer. In harmony with this law of sympathy, we find that it was sometimes through the faith of others, rather than that of the patient, that Jesus the Christ found a cure possible. Our individual minds, acting on a higher plane of thought, may be the medium of the transmission to him of the incipient idea of recovery, and our silent sphere may communicate to him a divine therapeutic *impression*, which will grow into a physiological impulse in the direction of health. A sympathetic friend, with his better thoughts and hopeful atmosphere and words of cheer, adds new fuel to the smouldering embers of my vital fire. His influence snuffs the candle burned down to a smoking wick. As a withered plant may absorb a reviving moisture from the air, so I receive new life from him. In treating a patient for the removal of the morbid idea in his mind, of which the disease is but the outward expression, I know of no better way than to form the true idea of him in my own mind, and set this over against his idea of himself. To one who, judging from the plane of sense, thinks himself sick, he is so to himself; but to one who, looking deeper, so as to find the *real man*, and thinks and knows that the true self is not diseased, to him the man is not sick. Here is a contest of ideas for the mastery, the old battle of Michael, the prince of God, the representative of the Christ-principle or of spirit on one side, and of the dragon on the other, the symbol of the principle of sense, the *nephesh*, the old serpent, reproduced on a smaller scale. Here it is an individual soul, rather than the world at large. (Rev. xii: 7–11.) But as our idea is spiritual, and his is on a lower plane, and as the higher by divine right governs the lower, the unequal contest is not doubtful. "The dragon and his angels fought, but prevailed not. And now is come the salvation, and the power, and the kingdom of our God, and the authority of his

Christ," for the accuser or deceiver (the principle of sense) is cast down. This old war between the spirit and the flesh is not always settled in a day, but if we form the true idea of ourselves and tenaciously maintain this mental position, he animal soul and its body will surrender to it in the end.

It is a doctrine taught in the ancient Hermetic philosophy, and the esoteric science of the East, that there is a *Universal Mind*. It is enough for our present purpose to say, that this Mind connects all individual minds in a state of sympathy It is the underlying philosophy of psychometry, or the susceptibility of being affected by the thoughts and feelings of others. For from this Universal Mind, or Greatest Man, as the Swedish seer denominates it, our minds are never separated, and through it our thought and will impulses are communicated to others, in a way analogous to that in which sound is supposed to be transmitted from one place to another through the atmosphere which unites them. Of this universal mind-principle, Emerson says, in the commencement of his Essay on History: " There is one mind common to all individual men. Every man is an inlet to the same, and to all of the same. He that is once admitted to the right of reason, is a freeman of the whole estate. What Plato has thought, he may think; what a saint has felt, he may feel; what has at any time befallen any man, he can understand. Who hath access to this universal mind is a party to all that is or can be done; for this is the only and sovereign agent. . . . Of this universal mind each individual is one more incarnation." (*Essays*, First Series, pp. 11, 12.)

Every man is not only an inlet of this universal mind, but may be an outlet of it. It not only flows into us, but our individual mind may be a channel through which it may go forth to bless and strengthen others, and that whether they are in the same room with us, or miles away; for in this universal principle distance is annihilated, and we may attain to that highest triumph of mind, *visio in distantia, et actio in distantia*, as Schopenhauer calls it, or vision and action independent of distance. For it is one of the deepest laws of our inner being, *that the spirit is always present with the object of thought, and that object tends to become one with it.* The mind of others is included in the general mind that comprises ours also in itself. Our will, faith, and imagination may transmit through it a beneficent and saving impulse, for no man is or can be alone. He is in vital and sympathetic conjunction with the whole realm of mind; as much so as the air in this room is not sundered from the air of immensity, and it may be renewed from it. It greatly increases our psychological and spiritual power in our efforts to do good and relieve human suffering, to feel that this universal mind (which, when uncontaminated by the general world-life, is the Holy Spirit) lies back of us as a reserved force, to be called into action when the occasion demands it. We should so consecrate ourselves to the good of universal being, that we may become an organ of communication between the Universal Divine Life and the diseased and unhappy one to whom we are called to minister. Says Dr. Wyld, in his excellent little book, "The wholesome, pure, and benevolent man or woman, by simply placing the hands on the patient, and calmly desiring the blessing of God, would seem to become sometimes a medium for the transmission of spiritual benevolence." (*Theosophy and the Higher Life*, p. 12.) There can be no doubt than it was the belief of the primitive and Apostolic Church, that a divine, sanative virtue and influence could be thus imparted to those who were receptive of it. If it were ever done in any age of the world, it can be done now as well.

By the power of silent suggestion, combined with a sincere *desire* to impart good and truth, and by vocal utterance if we deeply *feel* it, we can do much towards dislodging from the mind of an invalid the idea, the belief, the thought of his malady, and with the disappearance of this the body can be left to take care of itself, or rather it can be commended, like the plants of our garden, to the loving care of the Universal Life of nature. Our main point of attack should be on the morbid idea, for if this be expelled from its throne the sceptre will be taken by the higher soul, and convalescence will commence. Just as when a vessel has grounded on a dangerous sand-bar at the entrance of a harbor, by throwing over the useless ballast it will float of itself and by a law of its nature. So when the aeronaut finds himself descending into a swamp, he throws out a sand-bag, and he rises into a higher stratum of the atmosphere. By the power of silent thought, which in its nature is a *tacit speech*, we can deposit in the fruitful soil of the *unconscious mind* of an invalid the living germ of a better condition, which, like the mustard seed of Palestine, will develop into a tree. We may inoculate him with a sanative contagion. We may insert into his tree of life the bud, the living scion, that will unfold into a branch bearing better fruit. The spiritual nature of man acting through the will and imagination, and determined to a definite aim by love and faith, is the most *real force* in the universe, for thoughts are not "trifles light as air," but are substance and divinely living things. When an individual is in a passive, and consequently receptive, state, and is actuated by a sincere *desire* of recovery, he is highly sensitive to our thought and willimpulses, and these may affect the inner ground of his being. Though the impressions we make may not at the time be *felt* by him, they are undoubtedly *received*, and under the proper circumstances will manifest themselves in his improved condition. They are sometimes like characters written with invisible ink, which on exposure to the light and heat of the fire become plainly legible.

I would not give to the above a factitious value, like the advertisement of a patent nostrum, but may be allowed to say that after experiments with it for nearly a quarter of a century, in connection with the old *occult science of magnet-*

ism or the wisdom-lore of the ancient Magi, of which it is a part, I have found it to possess a therapeutic efficiency. There is no method (at least, I humbly confess after long and patient search I have not been able to find one) that will cure everybody and everything without regard to conditions, that sometimes lie beyond our control. Even Jesus, the Christ, did not and does not now scatter cures around him, like a royal prince throwing a handful of coin into a crowd of beggars. He cured the receptive few, and left the unreceptive many as they were. Nor is there any system of healing known to the most penetrating eye of spiritual science that can cure a man and leave him to live as he lists. This is a noxious medical heresy, at which we wish to hurl a passing rebuke, for it is either ignorance of all the laws that govern human life, or something worse. If the former, I take back the rebuke; if it be the latter, I let it stand. Nor is there any mental science of healing the ills that flesh is said to be heir to that a man can learn and successfully apply, irrespective of the degree of his mental attainments and spiritual development. It is possible to give to a student of spiritual philosophy only the alphabet, and he must *become* in himself all the rest. As the Rosicrucians of the days of old said, "the Rosie Cross becomes and is not made." And the needed spiritual evolution or unfolding is not the result of a single revolution of the earth on its axis, like the abnormal and unsubstantial growth of Jonah's gourd, but may be the slower and surer product of years. But I would not convey the impression that to become spiritual we must hide away from the world in the unapproachable solitude of mountains, or entomb ourselves alive within the barred enclosure of a monastery. Jesus did not this, and never recommended it. We may grow up with the world and in it, and not be of it.

To return to the subject of silent suggestion, we remark that it may be employed as an expression of faith in the treatment of ourselves. Based on the doctrine of the triune nature of man, and that the *pneuma* of the New Testament psychology and the Buddhi of the Hindu philosophy is divine, and that matter is an illusion, we ought to be able to *say in thought*, and to teach an invalid to say, I AM NOT SICK OR UNHAPPY. The disease is no more a part of myself than the mould on the plant is the same as the plant, or the barnacles on a ship are a part of the ship. The body is no more myself than the clothes I wear, and a rent, a stain, or a patch in my garment does not affect the man. But the truth of which the suggestion is the formulation, to be the most efficient, must *arise from within*. It then becomes the secret Logos, the Vach or sacred speech of the Vedas, the still small voice, the inaudible "word," and has a divine potency in it. This soundless word is the *Deus dixit*, the Lord said, of the Old Testament and of the Jewish prophets. It is the "lost word" which modern Masonry laments, and for which they try to find a substitute. It is that word or "ineffable name," through which, according to the belief of all nations, wonders were wrought, and which Jesus possessed in its perfection. The remarkable faith of the centurion consisted in his confidence in the saving power of this word. "Speak the *word* only, and my child (or servant) shall be healed." (Matt. viii: 5–10.) If we have not this inner or occult word, we do but little in the cure of disease by spiritual forces and agencies, and we must cover our face with a mantle and stand in the opening of the cave, as Elijah did, until it comes to us.

There is above us, and around us, and in us a realm of pure spirit, and inhabited by spiritual beings as much above our ordinary humanity that contributes to the swelling of the volume of the census as they are above the lower order of animals. It was a favorite conception of Plato that *thinking is asking*. Thought directed to the universal world of spirit becomes a silent interrogative impulse, and a response is echoed back in a spiritual idea or thought in our minds.

Hence the philosophical disquisitions of Plato took the dialogue form. If the reader should feel that thought addressed to this boundless realm of life is like speaking into vacancy, let him think of Jesus, and your cogitative aim has hit the central mark, for he, according to Paul, has been exalted to its summit and stands at its head. Through him as a point of contact we come into communion with the highest realm of life and thought. We drink at the fountain-head of pure spiritual knowledge. I cannot better close this somewhat protracted lesson than in the language of that noble man, Keshub Chunder Sen: " As pilgrims we approach the great saints, and commune with them in spirit, killing the distance of time and space. We enter into them, and they enter into us. In our souls we cherish them, and imbibe their character and principles. If they are not personally present with us, they may be spiritually drawn into our life and character. They may be made to live and grow in us. This is a normal psychological process, to which neither science nor theology need take exception. I believe philosophers have not noticed one thing, — the absorbent character of the soul. It is a wonderfully impressionable substance. An hour in the company of the saints is enough. The whole heart is revolutionized. All Scriptures bear testimony to this blessed influence." (*Oriental Christ*, by P. C. Mozoomdar, p. 128.)

> "Each creature holds an insular point in space,
>   Yet what man stirs a finger, breathes a sound;
>   But all the multitudinous beings round
>   In all the countless worlds, with time and place
>   For their conditions, down to the central base,
>   Thrill, haply, in vibration and rebound,
>   In full antiphony, by a common grace?
>   I think this sudden joyance, which illumines
>   A child's mouth sleeping, unaware, may run
>   From some soul newly loosened from earth's tombs.
>   I think, this passionate sigh, which half begun,

> I stifle back, may reach and stir the plumes
> Of God's calm angel standing in the sun."
>
> *(Mrs. Browning.)*

The universal spiritual realm of light and life is not reluctant to impart, but is waiting to give of its exhaustless stores as soon as we become admissive of its higher life. Jesus but gives voice to it when he says, "I have many things to say unto you; but ye are not able to bear them now. Howbeit, when he, the Spirit of truth, is come, he will guide you into all the truth." (John xvi: 12, 13.) The sole condition of receiving is a willingness to receive, and a disposition beneficently to use. Then by assuming an attitude of passivity, or mental inertia, toward it, we may *absorb* it, as the earth imbibes the light and heat of the sun.

CHAPTER XI.

WHAT IS IT TO BE SPIRITUAL? AND HOW MAY WE BECOME SO?

THERE is often in the minds of people only a vague idea of what it is to be spiritual. It is to them an indefinite something or "somewhat," which they are feeling round in the dark to find, and would hardly recognize it, even if they accidentally laid their hands upon it. It is among religious people usually confounded with a certain devotional frame of mind, and sometimes is viewed as an ecstatic state of the emotional nature. But these may exist, and the subject of those experiences may not have attained to the life of the spirit. They may be only the bubbles, painted by the sun with the hues of the rainbow, and floating on the current of the lower soul. What is it to be spiritual? how may I become so? are questions of the gravest practical importance to every human being. The great spiritual philosopher of the North answers the question by saying that, to think spiritually is to free thought from the limitations of time and space. In the Buddhistic philosophy, these inquiries are answered by teaching that to be spiritual is to be liberated from the bondage of *matter*. In the Christianity of Jesus, the inquiry is met with the answer, "Judge not according to *appearance* (ὄψις, sight, sense), but judge *righteous* judgment," which is the Sanscrit *rita*, the real truth. (John vii : 24.) This freedom from the bondage of matter and sense is to be accomplished not merely by ascetic mortifications, which are of no value except so far as they give us *self-control* in the fullest sense of the word, but by reaching a higher mental position, the standing-ground of *faith*, from which material things are seen and felt as illusions; that is, as an evanescent and deceptive appearance. To emancipate the mind from the fetters of sense, is to be free from disease and sin in the Platonic and New Testament signification of the word. This deliverance, together with the quenching of the lower desires, and a consecration to a life of love and use, is the Nirvana of Buddhism, and the kingdom of the heavens of Jesus. This can never be reached on earth (for it is a state attainable here and now), so long as we view matter as the most real thing in the universe. With this view as a confirmed and governing conviction, we can no more become spiritual than we can sail our ships of commerce in the air. In the most exalted moments of our religious life and feeling we are sometimes borne upward above the plane of sense, and earthly things seem vanity and delusion, "an empty show." But these experiences are often only transient moods, mere flashes of spiritual light in the starless darkness above and around us, instead of permanently established modes of thinking. In these ecstatic visions, which have no unshaken basis on which to rest, but are supported only by our ever-varying emotions, and a slender devotional framework, we soon again descend to the dead level of the plane of sense. Thus we alternately rise above the earth and sink into the dismal swamp of materialism. To be carried up by a mere devotional frame of mind, as in a balloon which is in constant danger of collapsing, is a very different position from that occupied by the man who has built his habitation and erected his observatory upon the summit of a mountain, which is an immovable point above the clouds, where the life of the heavens ever meets and mingles with our lower conditions. A philosophical idealism, of which Bishop Berkeley is one of the best exponents, when inwrought into the very texture of the mind, furnishes a secure and permanent foundation for a spiritual mode of thinking. It is the spontaneous philosophy of the interior man, as the current materialistic science is of the psychical or natural mind. The eagle is at home in the lofty atmospheric heights; the earth-worm is equally so in the mud; and both are useful in their proper place. "The great lesson," says Professor Fiske, "which Berkeley taught mankind was, that what we call material phenomena are really the products of consciousness coöperating with some Unknown Power (not material) existing beyond consciousness. We do very well to speak of 'matter' in common parlance, but all that the word really means is a group of qualities which have no existence apart from our minds. Modern philosophers have quite generally accepted this conclusion, and every attempt to overthrow Berkeley's reasoning has hitherto resulted in complete and disastrous failure. . . We are thus led to a view of things not very unlike the views entertained by Spinoza and Berkeley. We are led to the inference that what we call the material universe is but the manifestation of infinite Deity to our finite minds. Obviously, on this view, matter — the only thing to which materialists concede real existence — is simply an orderly phantasmagoria, and God and the soul, which the materialists regard as the fictions of the imagination, are the only conceptions that answer to real existences." (*Unseen World*, pp. 51, 52.)

When we come to a clear perception and intuitive conviction of this, a new and higher existence has dawned upon us. We have attained to the all-satisfying truth, and are made free. (John viii: 32.) In that day the interior soul of man has left the circumference of being, with all its unsubstantial shadows, and has moved up an immense distance toward the Central Life and Supreme Reality. Such a person is not of the world,. even as Jesus the Christ was not of the world. (John xvii: 14–16.) He can now act upon the body from within, as God perpetually operates in nature.

It is the doctrine of idealism that matter exists only in mind. This was the doctrine of Berkeley, Fitche, Hegel, and Emerson, and is well stated by Rev. Arthur Collier, a contemporary of Berkeley. In the introduction to the "Clavis Universalis," he observes: "I suppose I need not tell my reader that when I affirm that all matter exists in mind, after the same manner that body exists in place, I mean the very same as if I had said, that mind is the place of body, and so its place, as that it is not capable of existing in any other place, or in place after any other manner."

Matter, inclusive of the human body, exists for us only in the mind, and in the mind on the plane of sense, its lowest range of action. To elevate our consciousness above that basement story of our being, is to be clear of it. This is faith. We would ask the reader, If all your five senses were closed or were quiescent, would not matter to you be deprived of all its properties, and would there remain for you any external world or any physical body? The same is true of physical disease. It is the office of faith, as defined by Plato, and as the term is used by Jesus, to raise us to a higher plane of thought and perception, where disease as an external entity disappears. I would not affirm that to attain to this spiritual mode of thought is an easy acquirement, nor would I affirm that it is next to an impossible achievement to reach it. To apprehend it as theoretically true is not difficult. And most of us remain here *looking* up rather than *going* up. To the great mass of mankind, if they ever think of it at all, it is only a promised land seen in the distance from the mountain summit of our highest spiritual experiences. The humanity of Jesus climbed up to this celestial height, and also to some extent that of Gautama, the Buddha. Jesus, as an incarnation of the universal Christ, represents the whole of humanity, and hence he says, "If I be lifted up, I will draw all men unto me." (John xii: 32.) In the Grecian Mysteries, whose original aim was to lead the initiate from a mere external and sensuous plane of thought to the profoundest spiritual attainments, the fifth and last stage was denominated *friendship and interior communion with God*. This was the holy of holies of their spiritual temple, in which man reaches that summit of thought where there are but two truths in the universe, the All, and the nothing. Christianity aims to conduct its sincere disciples to the same goal, not by a mechanism of rites and ceremonies, nor by an unenlightened superstition and shallow enthusiasm, but by an orderly evolution of our spiritual nature. The nearer we approach it, the more our spiritual power and psychological force are augmented. It has been universally taught in the ancient spiritual philosophy, that the inmost soul of man is the outcome, or offspring, or offshoot, of the Universal Soul, and is a manifestation under finite limitations of the first creative Principle. If this is so (and it is intuitively true), then the inner nature of man must of necessity share in a degree the attributes of the world-creating Power. It is made into the image of God, and so far *is* God. We can form no idea of God that is not to some extent realized in us. The idea is in us and a part of us. We can worship no God that is not bounded by our conceptions, and we can conceive of nothing in Him that is not actually existent in the spiritual and divine powers which are either active or latent in us. The highest image we can form of Him is only what we are capable of becoming. I would not affirm that this is *all* of God, but only all that we can know of Him. Just so far as we know God, we become God, and can to the same extent do divine works.

As all matter exists only in mind, it follows that all modifications of the mind effect changes in *that appearance* which we call matter. This is an invariable law. The same object is never seen twice alike; as, for example, the ocean, the mountains, or the forest. Matter is an illusion or deceptive appearance that is perpetually changing with our ever-varying mental states. It is a sublime truth of the old philosophy, that the world is created through man, and everything in it corresponds to something in man. There is a close relationship between the life of the world and the life of man. We impress our character on our surroundings, or, to use a fashionable word, our environment. The latter does not make us, but we give character to it. It is said that when man fell, or descended from spirit to sense, the ground was cursed for his sake. So Milton says:

"Earth felt the wound, and nature sighing through all
Her works, gave signs of woe that all was lost."

As life is developed, the world is seen to be more and more. It is fair to suppose that the highest animal does not see as much in the world as we see. Take an idiot, and suppose him to rise in intellect until he becomes a sage; the earth keeps even pace with him. Suppose the sage gradually to sink into idiocy; the earth descends with him, becoming less and less, until it disappears. Hence the remark, so often made, that we shall die, but the world will live on, is not strictly true. The real truth is, the world will die, or become evanescent to our external senses, that is, the world that is in us, but we shall continue to live in a higher world, that goes forth from us, and through us. The same law holds good in regard to the relation of mind and body. The body is but a part of the external world, and both are to us what we think and believe them to be.

If we glance at our very ancient diagram, which symbolically represents the triune nature of man, the first triangle represents the spirit, as a personal limitation of the grand unity of spirit, and with its point downwards, its tendency to descend. It is masculine or active. The lower triangle represents the animal soul, which is considered in its relation to spirit as feminine or reactive, and in nearly all languages the word is feminine in form, as the Greek *psyche*, and the Latin *anima*. With the point upward it represents the tendency inherent in its nature, to ascend to meet the spirit. The union of the two, as in the two interlaced triangles, is significant of the highest condition of man on earth, the conjunction of the soul and spirit to form the interior man. The two triangles thus interlaced, are, according to Jacob Behmen, the highest religious symbol. It signifies not only the union of the spirit and soul, but also of God and man. The lower triangle, with its point upward, is aspiration, which meets a response in inspiration represented by the upper triangle with its point downward. The two together are the "Blazing Star," the "Star in the East," of the Magi, whose significance was fully realized in Jesus. They represent the true ideal state, the " celestial-natural " condition, as it was denominated by Swedenborg, the *true life of faith*, in which the higher light of the spirit perpetually corrects the illusions or deceptive appearances of the senses. Faith is not merely an intellectual state, but intellect in union with feeling, which is life, — life on a higher plane of thought. Belief and life, in their etymological sense, seem to be the same. To believe is to live, as the first syllable is only intensive, and the latter from the Danish *lever*, the German *leben*, the Dutch *lieven*, all meaning life or to live. To believe is a movement of our interior life towards the state which is the object of desire and of faith. To believe that we are well or are becoming so, turns the current of our life and of the Universal Life in that direction. To believe the truths of the spirit in opposition to the illusions of sense, is salvation in the complete signification of the word. These truths are the "blood of the Lamb," by which we overcome. (Rev. xii: 11.) It was a peculiarity of the old philosophy, that they expressed and preserved the highest truths under the covering of appropriate symbols. In the original zodiac, which signifies the circle or cycle of life, there were only ten signs, answering to the ten Sephiroth or emanations of the Kabala. The first was Aries the Lamb, and this answers to the Christ of Paul, the Universal Spirit. By the blood of the Lamb is therefore signified the living truths of the spirit, which is a meaning as fixed in the science of correspondence as the definitions of geometry. In this blood, which is perpetually shed for the many, we may wash our robes and make them white. It is this, and this alone, which can save the soul from its illusions, its sin, and disease. To save a man from bodily disease, without an effort to save the soul, is to act like a fireman who should rush into a burning building to rescue a sleeping inmate, and should only seize his clothes, and leave the man as he was. Not so did Jesus the Christ, who illustrates in his beneficent life the truth that the highest function of a healer is to be a *doctor* or teacher. And the highest and most saving truths we can dispense, are not those that we learn from books and teachers, but are the clear shining of the "Star in the East" within us. The Arabian alchemist, Abipili, utters these golden words: "I admonish thee, whoever thou art, that desirest to dive into the inmost parts of nature; if that thou seekest thou findest not *within* thee, thou wilt never find it *without* thee." When we act mentally upon an invalid or upon ourselves from the spiritual world within us, we act in concert with the intelligent forces that control nature, and can determine them to the healing of disease, or at least accelerate their action. It is the divine order that spirit should govern matter; or, as it was expressed in the ancient metaphysical science, that the heavens should rule. (Dan. iv: 26.)

The person who desires to become spiritual and acquire the power to cure disease by mental forces, in order to make money and become rich, has parted company with Jesus, and lost his way at the very commencement of his journey. He has switched off upon a side-track, and has accidentally stepped on board a freight train that is bound in the opposite direction, and has missed the passenger car which has moved on due *East*. He who desires to make money out of spiritual science, is like the man who vainly sighs for the wings of a dove that he might use them in wading in the mud. The wings of the soul of which Plato speaks are not given for that use. The truly spiritual man or mind does not desire to sell a minimum of spiritual truth for a maximum price in money; but rather imparts to all who will receive without money and without price. Spiritual gifts, among which is the gift of healing, God has never thrown into the markets of the world. The first recorded attempt to buy a spiritual gift was a disastrous failure, and the speculator in heavenly things purchased to himself only a severe rebuke. (Acts viii: 20.) To bring down the celestial life of the spirit into the disgusting scramble for wealth, is like inviting our angelic visitors to aid us in ditching our swamp. The most spiritual men the world has ever held, including Jesus, have been poor, in the ordinary sense of the word. But while poor in that sense, they possess all things. They may have no legal title to the land, but they own the whole landscape. They have in themselves as an everlasting inheritance all that the goodly things of earth spiritually signify and represent. They seek first the kingdom of God and its righteousness (right thinking), and all other things are thrown in, like the wrapping paper of the merchant. (Mat. vi: 33.) Gold and silver are symbols of celestial good and truth. Having in ourselves the latter we possess all that is of value in the former. This is the teaching of Jesus the Christ, and is Christian science and true metaphysics. This word was introduced into philosophy by Aristotle, and is composed of two Greek words which signify *after physics*. In a system of education, it was supposed that the study of physics, or of visible nature, came first, and the study of the spiritual side of nature and of the mind came last, or, as Paul expresses it, first that which is natural or psychical, then that which is spiritual. (I Cor. xv: 46.) To seek the achievement of spiritual development, in order to employ our powers in making money, is a total perversion of the divine order of life, and such a person becomes spiritually blind by an immutable law of our being. If we are now in the full light of the noonday sun, when the earth is fully inverted and we with it, we find ourselves in midnight darkness. So the spirit of man, which is full to overflowing of an irrepressible love and good will to all men, is the light side. The selfish animal soul is the dark side. We must see to it that our microcosm, or little world, does not turn bottom side up, but ever remain in its true position.

BE TRUE.

"Thou must be true thyself,
  If thou the truth wouldst teach;
Thy soul must overflow, if thou
  Another's soul wouldst reach;—
It needs the overflow of heart
  To give the lips full speech.

"Think truly, and thy thoughts
  Will the world's famine feed;
Speak truly, and each word of thine
  Will be a fruitful seed;
Live truly, and thy life will be
  A great and noble creed."

CHAPTER XII.

SPIRITUAL TRUTH THE BEST REMEDY FOR DISEASE.

As disease exists only on the mental plane of sense, as we have before shown, and this is the region in us which is subject to illusions and deceptive appearances, and as the disease itself for which we are often called to administer a remedy is in many cases only a sensuous seeming, so spiritual truth, which is only another name for faith, is the most efficient remedy in nature. It is a specific having a divine sanative virtue and potency in it. This should never be forgotten. Spiritual truth expresses the reality of things, or that which *is*, and when vocally expressed, or silently suggested and by a thought impulse projected into the mind of an invalid, is an infallible antidote to that *sin* (or error, or false belief), which is the underlying cause of disease, which is often unreal and in itself no-thing. In the case of a given disease, we are first to find out what is false and unreal in regard to it in the mind of the patient, and all this counts for nothing. It is a minus quantity. Subtract it from the diagnosis, and there is often no remainder — nothing which amounts to a concrete reality. Physicians frequently feel this, but may deem it inexpedient to say so. To ascertain what a so-called nervous patient *thinks* about his own case, is in nine cases out of ten the best statement of the sensuous delusions which are to be corrected. This he is only too willing to give us, and to pour it into the listening ear of every visitor. His statement of his condition is the one to be combated, and his confirmed ideas are to be expunged from his mind — not by reasoning merely, for that often only confirms him in them. His reason (so called) is the head of the serpent, that the seed of the woman, or the truths of wisdom, is to crush. Having heard his statement of the case, he should be instructed ever after to keep silent, as it is a law of our being, that to express a feeling in words gives intensity and fixedness to it. When I say "I am sick," my thought or existence is run into a different mould, from what it is when I say "I am well."

How a change in our mode of thought reaches the body through an intermediate form, organism, or medium, is told us by Swedenborg, which we quote not as an authority, but as an illustration. He says: "There was a philosopher who ranked among the more celebrated and sane, who died some years ago, with whom I discoursed concerning the degrees of life, and that one form is more interior than another, but that one exists and subsists from another; also that when an inferior or exterior form is dissolved, the superior or inferior form still lives. It was further said that all operations of the mind are variations of the form; in the purer substances these variations are in such perfection that they cannot be described; and that the ideas of thought are nothing else; and that these variations exist according to changes of the state of the affections. How the most perfect variations are given in the purer forms may be concluded from the lungs, which fold themselves variously, and vary their forms according to every expression of speech, every note of a tune, every motion of the body, *and according to every state of thought and affection;* what then must be the case with interior things which, in comparison with so large an organ, are in the most perfect state? The philosopher confirmed what was said, and declared that such things had been known to him when he lived in the world, and that the world should apply philosophical things to such uses, and should not be intent on bare forms of expression, and on disputes about them, and thus labor in the dust." (*Arcana Celestia*, 6326.)

According to this philosophy, when expressed more clearly, a change of thought — as an act of faith, or imagination, or any modification of the mind, on its higher plane — adjusts the form of the intellectual soul into its representative image, and this latter moulds the animal soul-principle and psychical body into its expression, and through this it passes outward to the physical organism. So a morbid and fixed idea forms the lower soul into its image, and this by a law of correspondence changes the outward body into a condition that expresses the idea on a material plane. Here it can go no further, as it has reached the outside boundary of existence. The term "body," in its radical sense, signifies that which is *fixed* or *set*. Hence the human body, in its different conditions, is always only the fixedness of an idea. This is also true of all matter, as all the endless variety of plants. They are divine ideas printed in the book of nature by the demiurgic intellect. So an act of faith, or a perception of spiritual truth, by supplanting the idea of disease, passes outward into a psychical or soul manifestation, and finally is translated into a bodily expression. Since every idea of the mind forms the soul and interior body, which are the inward man, into its expression, it has been affirmed, and is eternally true, that in the other life, as we call it, the whole quality of a man is exquisitely perceived from a single idea of his thought, for every idea is an image of the man. (*Arcana Celestia*, 301.) And by those whose inner vision is unveiled, and who have emancipated the intellectual soul from the body, the same can be seen now. When the Christ as the primal Light and Life comes to a man, — and he may come every day and not merely at the end of the world to us, — the veil of sense is removed.

> "He comes from thickest films of vice,
>   To clear the mental ray,
> And on the orbs oppressed with night,
>   To pour celestial day."

If we have a man's ruling idea and his central love, we have the whole man, all that he is or can be for the time being; for all his thoughts and feelings revolve around these, and never break entirely loose from their orbit. Hence Emerson very truly says, "The key to every man is his thought. Sturdy and defying though he look, he has a helm which he obeys, which is the idea after which all his facts are classified. He can only be reformed by showing him a new idea which commands his own." (*Essays, First Series,* p. 241.) In having your picture taken, the artist always recommends you to have some pleasant thought in your mind, because this gives you the best expression. But thought affects not only the face, but the whole body. Would it not be well for some nervous invalids to sit for their picture several times a day, until they become themselves the fixed and finished picture of their pleasant thought? "Every distinct idea of man, and every particular affection, is an image and effigy of him, even as to its minutest fraction; that is, there is something therein which partakes, in a nearer or remote degree, of all his intellect and of all his will" (or love). (*Heavenly Secrets,* 803.) A man's ruling idea, to the inner eye, is a spiritual image of the real man, far more so than our picture taken by the photographic artist is a representation of ourselves. For in the one there is life, while the other is but an inanimate shadow. But we must never lose sight of this deep law of our being, *that all ideas have an inherent tendency to actualize or externalize themselves in the corporeal organism.*

The science of modern times has never appreciated the power of intense *thought* directed to a person with a beneficent end or healing intention. Medical science admits the influence of the imagination of a patient upon himself, but wholly ignores the influence of our imagination and faith upon others, which is by no means an unimportant matter. The mind can thus act at any distance. In the realm of spirit, thought is a movement (so to speak) of the spirit, a transportation or extension of the spirit, a being "carried away in the spirit" to the place or person that is the object of thought. Our inner being accompanies its thought, so that wherever the thought is, there the spirit is, and there it can act; for it is the spirit that thinks, and its thought is inseparable from it. This fact is recognized by Charlotte Brontë, and illustrated in her novel of "Jane Eyre." She makes her heroine hear the voice of her lover, calling her name, though they were far apart in space; and she was so strongly impressed with its reality that she leaves all and goes to him, finds him blind and suffering, and needing her love and sympathy, and really calling her in *spirit*. Such a phenomenon is not wholly a fiction, and much less a miracle. It comes within the domain of the laws of the mind. Such mental telegraphy is an every-day occurrence among the true adepts of spiritual philosophy.

The proclamation of the *spiritual* truth in regard to a given malady, will have more effect in removing its cause and weakening its hold, than the whole list of drugs described in the United States Dispensatory. Few diseases can long withstand the light of truth, but will silently disappear before it like birds of night at the approach of day, or like the mists of the morning before the rising sun. The man who habitually occupies the idealistic and spiritual plane of thought, and can speak with confidence from that commanding position, can say with Jesus, "The words that I speak unto you are spirit and are life." (John vi: 63.) And his utterances or *tacit affirmations* addressed to the patient will have a sanative and redeeming potency far beyond the prescriptions of the superficial learning of the medical schools, though I would not undervalue a true medical science.

The advantage we gain in speaking to a patient in thought rather than by vocal utterance, is that in the former case we are met by no opposition of will, no tendency to question and raise objections, and what we thus say to him reaches the interior degree of his being, whereas a verbal utterance may penetrate no further than the external plane of his mind, or even lodge in the external ear. The arrow of truth falls into the morass, and does not pass to the flowery fields beyond. When we speak to a patient in thought and *in silent prayer*, we touch the hidden spring of his life if he is in a condition of receptivity, and thus filter the stream at its fountain. We can thus act upon him independent of distance and all material limitations and restraints, if we have learned to speak the inner language. In the system of Jesus, as sin, in the sense of an error or fallacious *idea* (and not merely what we call wickedness, for in the original that is expressed by another word), in the mind, was recognized as the cause of disease and as constituting its spiritual essence, so truth was deemed to possess the highest therapeutic efficacy. This is to be spoken in love, according to the direction of Paul (Eph. iv:15), and in the same spirit we should tenaciously adhere to it. Such truth is not an empty abstraction or "airy nothingness," but the most vitally real and potential thing in the universe. It inherits God's loving omnipotence, from whom it is perpetually born. All forces are spiritual, and a spiritual truth is a divine force. As Paul asserts, "we can do nothing against the truth." (II Cor. xiii:8.) That will hold its own against all odds, and in the end have everything its own way. Single-handed and alone, it is more than a match in its silent omnipotence against a noisy mob of delusions. In dispensing truth as a curative agency we are not dealing in empty abstractions (for truth is never sundered from the Divine Mind), nor in the infinitesimal triturations of matter, but in the divinest and most substantial force in the whole realm of nature.

There is a marvellous power in a living thought, especially when it proceeds from the theocentric region of our being; and this power is becoming recognized by science. Says J. H. Stirling (the translator and commentator of Hegel) in his triumphant reply to Huxley's "Physical Basis of Life," "Throughout the entire universe *thought* is the controlling sovereign, nor does matter anywhere refuse its allegiance. So it is in thought too that man has his patent of nobility, and believes that he is created in the image of God, and himself a freeman of infinitude." (*Half Hours with Modern Scientists*, p. 125.) A friend of ours, a physician of Boston, in a letter, writes, "It occurred to me a short time since that we should think well of all, and not ill of any, because the thought of another has some power to make him what we think him, not only physically but morally. Momentous realities are involved in our thoughts. How little of such realities are realized by the majority."

He who has attained to the power of spiritual thought has been anointed and crowned a king. This is the Kabalistic "crown of life." The ruling idea of the minds of such men as Appolonius of Tyana, who was, I think, nearly contemporary with Jesus, was the rightful sovereignty of the spirit, the supreme and real man, over all below it in the scale of life. (Gen. i: 26–28.) An intelligent apprehension of this truth, and the *feeling* of it gave him his marvellous power, as it did also to Pythagoras and to Jesus. Such men are not mere spectators of nature, mere lookers on, but control it and make it subservient to their will. Jesus was a king (John xviii: 36–38), and so is every man in the unseen depths of his spirit, wherein lies the image or idea of God. But it is of little use to be a king and not know it. To have the sovereign power of spirit, and not to know it or be conscious of it, is all the same as not to have it. And we can know it only by faith, which is "the evidence of things not seen."

On the sovereign power of the mind, Dr. Nichols, a distinguished chemist, very truly and eloquently says, "The mind of man is the great overpowering force in the world, a principle dominating everything. No form of energy acting under law has escaped its control, no physical forces have become its master; they all combined bow to its behests and become its servants. It must be a supernatural principle, a distinct creation, a divine essence, a mighty force, standing apart, and designed to stand apart, from all the other forces of nature." (*Whence? What? and Where?* By James R. Nichols, M.D., p. 12.)

The inquiry will be raised, "Of what use is it to think the real truth of a person unless he is influenced to think the same of himself?" In answer to this, let it be observed that thought spontaneously takes a fixed form in an idea, which is a thing of life. When we think of a patient near or far off in space, if we think spiritually or *in a state of abstraction from the body*, and hold steadfastly to our thought of him, it will be transferred to him if he is receptive, and will assume form in his mind as an idea the same as in ours. If we recognize the truth that his spiritual and real self, the immortal Ego, is not sick or unhappy, the thought will take form in his mind as an idea and *belief*, and this makes it to him a reality so long as the idea and belief remain. Swedenborg affirms that when an angel of heaven determines his sight, that is, his thought, to another, his interiors are transferred and communicated to him according to his state of receptivity. (*Heavenly Secrets*, 10,130.) The same is true of our spirit, or of man as a spirit. When we think of a person the real truth in regard to him, that the real self is not invaded by disease, and think this with a feeling of its truth and with a beneficent desire to do him good, our "interiors" are transferred to him through the medium of the universal mind, and he thinks from us, but all the time not knowing otherwise than that he thinks wholly from himself. The thought will arise in him, "I am not sick." He is, in a certain true sense, *inspired* by us, and caused to think and feel above his ordinary level. This supplies the missing link that connects our thinking with the mind of the patient, which we shall more fully illustrate in our instruction regarding the universal life-principle. We often witness through the operation of this occult law two or more persons in the same room who are found to have been thinking of the same object or person at one and the same time. So all the great discoveries and inventions have been made by men in different parts of the world at about the same time. Our thoughts and ideas are recorded on the imperishable tablet of the universal intellect, and through this become contagious. This is a principle of the Hermetic philosophy, which has more influence on human life and its manifestations than has been recognized by modern science.

It is to be observed that the powers of the soul increase in proportion as it is freed from the influence of the body. The intermediate or intellectual soul can be affected either by the higher spirit or by the lower animal soul and the body, as was taught by Plato. And to teach the initiate how to liberate the soul from the body and set it free from the distorting influence of the senses was one of the aims of the esoteric science of the ancients, — a subject to which we shall recur in our next lesson. The potency of the will and the imagination in a state of ecstasy was an idea familiar to the old occult philosophy, and is mentioned by Paracelsus and Van Helmont, the fathers of modern magnetic science. But the state which was called by the Neo-Platonists ecstasy is not necessarily an abnormal one, but is in reality only the intellectual soul acting independent of the body. There are persons who can enter into this condition at will, and act from a higher or interior degree of the mind, and thus be "endued with power from on high."

CHAPTER XIII.

ON THE TRIUNE NATURE OF MAN, AND THE FREEING THE SOUL FROM THE BODY.

THE doctrine of the triune nature of man is one of the oldest doctrines of philosophy, and is absolutely fundamental in a true spiritual science. It was an occult doctrine, and was revealed in the fullest degree only to the highest initiates, or the "perfect," as they are called by the apostle Paul. In the Kabala man is viewed under the three divisions, or distinct regions, of mental being, named spirit, soul (ruach), and *crude spirit* (nephesh). The latter is the "serpent" of Genesis, and designates the principle of sense, and the mere animal mind or man. The body was very properly viewed as no part of man, as all its elements belong to the so-called external world. Man is identical with mind, as the term is from a Sanscrit word meaning to think. Man is mind; and each degree of the mind is man as he thinks and acts on either of three discrete planes of being.

In the Platonic philosophy, — which professedly was borrowed from the arcane science and religion of India, Egypt, and the East, — man, or mind, is viewed under the three degrees of *pneuma* (spirit), *psyche* (soul), and *thumos* (animal and irrational soul). The spirit, sometimes called *nous*, was considered as the real man, or man as he exists in the divine idea; and as it is generated by the Father (pure thought), and is the first emanation from the "Unknown," it possesses a nature kindred and even homogeneous with the Divinity, and is capable of beholding the eternal realities. The lowest degree is the blind animal life-principle, or soul, technically called *thumos*. The word is derived from the verb θύω (*thuo*), meaning to burn and also to sacrifice. It means, also, to move with a rapid, violent, impetuous motion, and hence was considered the seat of all disordered and vehement passions, such as govern the life of animals. In the New Testament Psychology it is called the flesh and the carnal mind, and to be under its dominion is death. It is the sensuous mind, the seat of all sensation, as many animals have the senses more acutely developed than man. All its perceptions are illusory and fallacious, — a false seeming. Life on this plane, the basement story of conscious being, is a dream, rather than a reality, when the innermost divine spirit is latent, and not developed into conscious activity. Plato, in the "Republic," represents such men as captives in a subterranean cave, with their backs turned toward the light, and who can see nothing but the reflected shadows of things, and yet think them actual realities. In order to the perception of the real truth of things, we must rise to a higher plane of thought and life.

The intermediate degree, or distinct region of mind, which is situated between the two extremes of mental existence, and which is capable of being influenced by either the higher or the lower, — the inmost divine spirit or the irrational animal soul, — was called *psyche*, or the rational soul. When freed from the distorting influences of the physical senses and the selfish animal passions, and disencumbered of the body, it is the Logos or Word, — the true light of every man that cometh into the world. It dwells in the "intelligible world," — the world of ideas and of enduring realities. It is the region of creation and of formation. It is the true object of all education to free the soul from the trammels of the body, and raise it from the plane of sense to the perception of the real and the enduring, in the place of the mere seeming, the ever-changing, and the evanescent. This is the liberty wherewith the Christ, the inward Word, makes us free (Gal. v: 1). It is the "Justice," or right thinking of the Kabala, a rectitude of mental perception, called by the apostle Paul the righteousness which is of faith. For faith is the action of the mind above the plane of sense.

Swedenborg's doctrine of degrees, or of three discrete regions of the mind, was borrowed and reproduced from the Hermetic philosophy. He says: "In every man there are from creation three degrees of life, — the celestial, the spiritual, and the natural." (*True Christian Religion*, sec. 239.) These degrees constitute three distinct ranges or planes of life, or three worlds or heavens. In another place, Swedenborg says: "I have been instructed concerning these degrees of life, that it is the last degree of life which is called the external or natural man, by which degree man is like the animals as to concupiscences and phantasies. And that the next degree of life is what is called the internal and rational man, by which man is superior to the animals; for by virtue thereof he can think and will what is good and true, and have dominion over the natural man by restraining and also rejecting its concupiscences and the phantasies thence derived; and moreover, by reflecting within himself concerning heaven, — yea, concerning the Divine Being, — which the brute animals are altogether incapable of doing. And that the third degree of life is what is most unknown to man, although it is that through which the Lord flows into the rational mind, thus giving man a faculty of thinking as a man, and also conscience, and a perception of what is good, and elevation from the Lord towards Himself. But these things are remote from the ideas of the learned of our age." (*Arcana Celestia*, 3747.) This doctrine of degrees bears a close resemblance to the Platonic views given above.

The Alchemists, who were simply Hermetic philosophers, writing in a language wholly unintelligible to those who had not the key to it, made the trine nature of man and all things to consist of *salt*, *mercury*, and *sulphur*. Salt was the universal menstruum, the *prima materia*, from which all concrete things spring, and to which they are reducible, and is the body of man as to its primal substance. Mercury was the symbol of the rational soul, the true *anima mundi*, the Logos, or creative Word in man. Sulphur was the secret fire or spirit in the system of the Alchemists. The three united into a unity, which is the true spiritual or illuminated state, was the philosopher's stone, and the white stone of the Apocalypse. (Rev. ii : 17.) It was the true magic mirror or translucent "spirit-seeing crystal." The term for crystal in Greek is, when divided into twin or half-words as follows: chryst-allos, and means that the philosopher's stone is the Christ within, in whom are hid all the treasures of wisdom and knowledge. Christ within is the great mystery of the Gospel. (Col. i : 27.) "Know," says Synesius, "that the *quint*-essence and hidden thing of our 'stone' is nothing less than our celestial and glorious soul, drawn by our magistery (instruction) out of its mine, which engenders itself, and brings itself forth."

Dr. Justinus Kerner, in his life of Madam Haufe, the Seeress of Prevorst, following the Kabala, makes our inner man to consist of *geist* (spirit), *seele*, (soul), and *nerven geist*, or *nerve spirit*, a semi-intelligent life-principle. The *nerven geist* answers to the Kabalistic *nephesh, crude spirit*, and being only of a semi-spiritual nature, is that which renders the rational soul visible as an apparition. It is the astral body, and by means of it the soul is enabled to affect material objects, make noises, and move articles. In short, it can speak to the inner ear of a person, using the universal æther as its vibrating atmosphere. *The adept or true illuminatus can free his soul from the body at any time*, for he has attained to the liberty of the sons of God (Rom. viii : 21), and can clothe the soul with the more subtle elements of the *crude spirit* or *nephesh*, and go where he pleases, and produce effects, as interiorly speaking to a person communicating to them an idea and an inward impulse to an action, imparting to them a sense of his presence, and sometimes becoming visible to them. In this state a man is invested with the powers and properties of a disembodied spirit, and can speak by psychological impression to another mind *far or near*. Says the northern Seer, "The speech of an angel or of a spirit with man is heard as sonorously as the speech of one man with another, *yet it is not heard by others who stand near*, but by the man himself alone. The reason is that the speech of an angel or of a spirit flows first into the man's thought, and by an internal way into his organ of hearing, and thus actuates it from within; whereas the speech of man flows first into the air, and by an external way into his organ of hearing, which it actuates *from without*. Hence it is evident that the speech of an angel and of a spirit with man is *heard in man*, and since it equally affects the organs of hearing, that it is equally sonorous."

It was one of the arcane principles of the archaic wisdom religion and science of man, that is now lost to the world at large, that it is possible for the intellectual soul to free itself from the trammels of the body, and emancipate itself from all material restraints and limitations. It then acts above time and space, and can transport itself, *with all its senses*, to any part of the world, guided and governed by the inner divine *pneuma* or *spirit*. It can make itself *felt* and *seen* by persons a hundred miles away, for it is where it *thinks* to be. In the tenth book of the Pymander (power of thought divine) of Hermes, it is said: "Command thy soul to go to India, and sooner than thou canst bid it, it will be there."

"Bid it likewise pass over the *ocean*, and suddenly it will be there."

"Command it to fly into *heaven*, and it will need no wings, neither shall anything hinder it, not the fire of the sun, nor the æther, nor the turning of the spheres; not the bodies of any of the stars;—but, cutting through all, it will fly up to the last and furtherest body."

If any one should ask, "What becomes of the body, while the soul is absent from it?" the answer is that its life is continued and all the vital processes are carried on by the Universal Soul, of which the individual soul is a part.

This separation of the soul, and making it independent of the body and of the laws of matter, can be done when the person is in a perfectly normal state, without a trance, and only in a state of mental abstraction, which would not be noticed by others; or, as Swedenborg calls it, "in a state of perfect wakefulness."

It would at first thought appear, that to free the soul from the body was the last thing reached, in our spiritual development, the very summit of human attainment. But so far is this from being the case, that it is viewed in the Hermetic philosophy as the first step to a true spiritual elevation, and the evolution of the deific powers of man. It is to be observed, as Thomas Taylor has remarked in the preface to his translation of the "Phædo" of Plato, that to separate the soul from the body, that is, to set it free from the limitations of the bodily senses, and disencumber it of all gross matter, is one thing, and to separate the body from the soul is quite another thing. The one is a philosophical state, the other is what men call natural death. To be able to emancipate the soul, and free it from all dependence upon organic conditions, is necessary to the highest form of knowledge and spiritual power. Plato says in the "Phædo": "It is demonstrated to us, that if we are designed to know anything purely, we must be liberated from the body, and behold things with the soul itself." When we do this we become inhabitants of an interior realm, the "intelligible world," the home of all knowledge, and see things in *idea* alone, and consequently in their reality. Freed from the earthly body, the soul appears in that world in a form or body that is composed of the pure substance of that world. "For according to the *arcana* of the Platonic philosophy," says Thomas Taylor, "between an etherial body, which is simple and immaterial, and is the eternal connate vehicle of the soul, and a terrene (or earthy) body, which is material and composite, there is an aerial body, which is material indeed (like the *nerven geist* of Kerner, and the *nephesh* of the Kabala), but simple, and of a more extended duration. And in this body the unpurified soul dwells for a long time after its exit from hence, till this pneumatic (or aerial) vehicle being dissolved, it is again invested with a composite body; while, on the contrary, the purified soul immediately ascends into the celestial regions with its etherial vehicle alone." Plato, in the "Cratylus," a treatise on the "rectitude of names," says that the body ($\sigma\hat{\omega}\mu\alpha$) of man was so named because it is the sepulchre ($\sigma\hat{\eta}\mu\alpha$) of the soul. And it was the object of the Eleusinian Mysteries to show that union with the body and bondage to matter and sense, was death. This was taught also by Jesus and Paul. To free the soul from its material thraldom, and convince it of the *illusory* nature of matter, is the true *anastasis*, or resurrection of the soul from the dead. This is the resurrection to which Paul refers, and which he sought to attain. (Phil. iii: 11–13.) It was the aim of Buddhism, and also of the ancient Mysteries, to lead the initiate to this. To this Jesus refers when he says, " Ye shall know the truth, and the truth shall make you free." (John viii: 32.) It is the state of *ecstasy* of Plotinus and the Neo-Platonists, and which they considered necessary to the attainment of the most exalted spiritual knowledge and power. It is a state in which the ordinary functions of the senses are suspended, and the pure mind is freed from their dominion. Says the Kabala, "Come and see when the soul reaches that place which is called the Treasury of Life; she enjoys a bright and luminous mirror, which receives its light from the highest heavens." (*Sohar*, I, 65, *b*.) In closing this section, I would only say that the Rosicrucians claimed to be able to know all that was ever known in any part of the world and in every age; for all that was ever known still exists, indelibly recorded on the tablet of the Universal Mind, and our individual mind may be an inlet to it. All that was ever known exists in the "intelligible world," the world of *ideas;* and into this realm we rise when we learn to forget the body and become spirit.

The action of the intellectual soul at a distance, and an internal *perception* of persons and things, which is not dependent upon the external organs of sense, which is sometimes witnessed in the present day, is no new phenomenon in psychological science. It was experienced by Paul, and hence belongs to Christianity, and is nothing foreign and hostile to it. He says to the Christians at Colosse, "Though I am absent in the flesh, yet am I with you in the spirit, joying and *beholding* your order and the steadfastness of your faith in Christ." (Col. ii: 5.) To the same effect he speaks to the Corinthian Church. (I Cor. v: 3.) And also the remarkable experience recorded in II Cor. xii: 1–5. These states were only a liberation of the soul from the trammels of matter, and not a projection of the soul out of the body, as some have called it, for that would imply that the soul was in the body like a bird in a cage. This is not the real truth, but an illusion as much as the appearance of our image *in* a mirror, which is not in the glass at all, but in our sensorium, which is the mind on the plane of sense.

CHAPTER XIV.

EXECUTING JUDGMENT UPON OURSELVES, OR IN THOUGHT SEPARATING DISEASE FROM THE REAL SELF.

To think and to exist are one and the same. *I think* and *I am* are identical expressions. To think rightly is to be well and happy. The first thing to be done in curing ourselves of disease by the ideal or psychological method, is to separate, in thought, our inner conscious self, the immortal divine *Ego*, from the disease, placing the malady outside our real being, and viewing it as no part of ourselves, but as something foreign to us. This, in the expressive language of Scripture, is executing a judgment, or an act of separation, as the word means, upon ourselves. We learn to *distinguish* between ourselves and the disease. Of disease and pain, which seem to be the common lot of mankind, Fichte very truly says: "They can reach only the nature with which I am in a wonderful manner united, not what is properly myself, the being exalted above nature." (*Destination of Man*, p. 125.) Supposing I had a wart upon my hand; I should ask myself the question, is that wart any necessary part even of my body? I am certain that it is not, but is rather a superfluous and needless excrescence. But I am equally conscious that it is no part of my inner self, — what Plato, and Paul, and Swedenborg call the inward man. The same is true of disease, which is always a deformity, or a deviation from the true idea of my being. It is no part of my real self. I disown and renounce all connection with it, and relationship to it. If I can maintain this attitude of thought toward it, the malady will disappear as certainly as a cloudy day will sometime be followed by sunshine. It will have no solid foundation on which it can rest, and will vanish as surely as the loosened hair of an animal in spring will fall from him, or the withered, and now useless, leaves in autumn will drop from the tree to the ground.

Of one truth we may be certain, and it is fundamental in the ideal or transcendental method of healing ourselves or others: that what I do not *like* is no part of *me*. Jesus said of the prince of the world, or the ruling principle of the age in which he lived, that it came to him, but found nothing in him. There was nothing in him that responded to it. He executed judgment upon it, and separated himself wholly from it. "Now is the judgment of this world (or age). Now shall the prince of this world (or age) be cast out." He elevated himself above and out of the current or sphere of the world-life. Paul also learned from the profound occult philosophy and arcane science into which he had been initiated, to distinguish, or separate in thought, between his real self, his spiritual entity, and what he did not like, or that to which his ruling love and his will, which were his life, were opposed. He says: "The good that I would (or desire) I do not; but the evil that I would not, that I do. Now if I do that I would not (or dislike), it is no more I (the true self) that do it, but sin (in the sense of error, illusion) that dwelleth in me." (Rom. vii: 19, 20.) This is a most important principle, and of far-reaching practical value. Let us return to our rude illustration of disease, the wart on the hand, or we can take a tumor internal or external. If I *like* it, I take it up into my life, and it becomes an integral part of myself. I incorporate it into my being, and I become one with it. This is true of everything I like. It finds something in me that responds to it, and which meets and unites with it. In fact, it is only the outward correspondence of what was already in me. But if I do not like it, and thus view it as something foreign to me, I separate it from my life, and the wart, or tumor, or disease will die, and I shall live on without it. If I thus disown it as a part of myself, and cease to think of it as included in the contents of the *Ego*, it will derive no support from my inner being, and will disappear as certainly as a branch severed from a tree will wither and die of itself. So a disease upon which I sit in judgment, from the throne of the divine spirit in me, or which I separate from my conscious inner self, and utterly disown as a part of myself, will be not only like a house built upon the sand, but like a castle in the air, a building that has no foundation, and which must of necessity fall to the ground, or rather must be viewed like all sensuous illusions as having no real existence. We make disease a part of ourselves only by *thinking* it such, and thus we give it vitality, and a certain hold upon us. This is a falsity, a phantasy, an error, an illusion, and a *sin* in the New Testament and proper sense of the word. The great lesson which every invalid needs to learn, is to cast it out of his real inner self, by viewing that self as entirely distinct and separate from it, to draw, as it were, a circle to represent his inward man, his spiritual being, and then place the disease as an unsightly blot outside its circumference. Disease is thus no longer classed with the realities of being, but is relegated to the region of illusion. By a right mode of thinking we cast it out and dispossess ourselves of it. Then it will be as the poet Crabbe says of every great lie — like a great fish out of water. Only let it alone, and it will die of itself. When I am conscious that I do not *like* a disease that has afflicted me, then that inward self that dislikes it may be considered as entirely free from it. It is outside the boundaries of my immortal and real being. To maintain with a volitional obstinacy this attitude of thought towards it, will have a marvellous power in curing it. By coming to a rectitude of judgment, as Jesus calls it, and elevating our thoughts above the region of a false seeming, it removes the obstruction in the way of the inward divine self, appropriating the physical organism as its perfect representative in the world of sense. If we steadfastly hold in mind this true idea of ourselves, it will form the soul, and through that the body into its outward expression, just as certainly as in a stormy day, when the clouds are dispersed, the sun will shine. The error, the illusion, that *I* am sick, or in pain, or any discomfort, that my real and inner self is diseased or unhappy, is that alone which forms a cloud between me and the sun of a higher sky, whence all life emanates. When that veil is removed, the Sun of Righteousness with its living light will arise within my interior world *with healing on its wings*. The chilling fog of sensuous fallacies and delusions will lift, and show our willing feet the shining pathway to a higher life and diviner blessedness.

It is to be kept in mind that all natural objects have an immaterial or spiritual side which is their invisible counterpart. This is their image or idea. All the things of the outward world — the sun, moon and stars, rivers, trees, mountains and flowers — have existence in mind alone, as thoughts and feelings, or ideas and sensations. If either is wanting, they cease to exist as concrete entities. For, as Berkeley affirms, their *esse* is *percipi;* that is, their being consists in being perceived. The same is true of the human body and those conditions of it which we call diseases, as a wart, or tumor, or cancer. These are but a combination of sensational images or ideas, apart from which they cannot have an objective reality.

We have shown in what has been said above the importance of separating our inner self from the malady of whatever nature it may be, and of viewing our real self as free from it. For, as Von Meyer's lucid subject says, "The spirit is not subject to suffering as the soul is," and the spirit is what we mean by the *Ego*, when we say *I am*. But we may go a step further in this act of judgment, and disown the very *idea* of disease. The disease, according to the system of Berkeley, exists only as a morbid idea, and this has an existence only in the external sensuous range of mind, the animal soul, or Paul's *psychical* man. This is not my divine and immortal *Ego* or self, for that is spirit, and as such is a manifestation of the grand unity of Spirit, which is God. This is the Kabalistic "Son of God." It was taught by Hermes Trismegistus, that God's Son is the only *man*, and is the immortal divine spirit that constitutes the inmost being of every personality. It is the divine entity which is the *real man*, the essential *Ego*, for the material body, and its vivifying animal soul are only the covering of the real man. And this divine personality is exempt from the possibility of old age, disease, pain, and death itself. By disowning and renouncing the *idea* of the malady as being any part of our real self, it will fade away from thought and existence, because we have cut the root from which it derives all its life. We say of certain persons that we dislike the sight of them, and even renounce the thought of them. We disown them as companions, cut ourselves loose from their society, and throw away and burn their picture, and everything which can by association recall their idea. With a calm and tranquil frame of mind we must do something like this with disease, and pain, and the source of any mental unhappiness. We must learn to separate our real self, the immortal "Son of God," from it, and renounce all ownership in it as a part of ourself, and then do the same with the sensational image or idea of it in the soul, which is the sensuous or animal mind, and the only seat of disease and pain. We view this *thumetic* region of our existence with all its contents of disordered passions, phantasies, illusions, and morbid ideas, as outside the circumference of our *inner divine self*. This is the dividing asunder of the soul and spirit under the influence of the inward divine light, which is called the Word of God, of which the unknown author of the Epistle to the Hebrews speaks. (Heb. iv: 12.) He, who can learn to do this with facility, has a marvellous power of healing himself and others. It is the highest act of faith, and that state of mind to which Jesus refers when he says: "Be it unto thee according to thy faith." Faith is an activity of mind above the plane of the senses, and a perception of truth that lies above and beyond their illusions and fallacious appearances. It is the divine order that the higher should control the lower; the interior, the external. And as faith springs from the inmost divine realm of our being, since it is, as Paul asserts, "the gift of God," it has dominion *dei gratia* over both the soul and the body.

CHAPTER XV.

THE CREATIVE POWER OF THE IDEAL, OR THE EXTERNALIZATION OF THOUGHT.

In the Kabalistic scheme of creation, called the ten *Sephiroth*, or Emanations, and which contains the key to all arcane philosophy, the first emanation from the "Unknown" is *pure thought*. This is the Christ of whom Paul so often speaks, the starting-point, the Crown of all existence. This divides into two rays, — a Father and Mother ray: a masculine and active, a feminine and reactive potency; the one pure intelligence, the other wisdom. The union of these in all their correlations is necessary to the existence of everything in earth and heaven. Existence and thought are identical. All being (or substance) by a law of necessity assumes *form*. A thought of a thing, by a law of evolution inherent in its nature, assumes form in an *idea*, which is the living image of the thought. It is the form, or first *expression*, of the thought. But an idea tends to a further externalization, in fact, to become an actuality in the world of sense. This is the true conception of the law of creation. It is the successive stages in the externalization of thought, first as a living image or soul of a thing which we call an idea. It is being, or thought, becoming visible in a *form* and as a form. Then it passes still further outward (or downward) and ultimates itself in the material world, or comes to a manifestation on the plane of sense. All mind is essentially creative, and the subjective tends to become objective, and the ideal to pass into the actual. As God creates the world by that effort of Will and Thought, — which Plato calls the Divine Idea, and Swedenborg and the Gospel of John, the Word, — so we, as being in the image of God, can, in a certain proper sense, create. With a certain intensity of will and thought, the images that arise are subjective. They are called hallucinations, or creatures of the imagination. They are by no means destitute of reality, for all the objects of nature are only a mental picture more or less vivid. To us, as in our dreams, they are as real as any of the visible objects of the world around us. With a more intense and intelligent concentration of the will, the intellectual ideas take shape in the *cosmic matter*, — the mother principle of things, — and become concrete, objective, and visible entities. Here is the greatest of secrets, the deepest of all mysteries, explained, — the law of creation. In this way God perpetually creates the world in us and through us.

All ideas distinctly formed in the mind respecting ourselves tend to a full realization in the body. The spiritual and ideal form tends to a further externalization in a material shape. The condition of the body is always the material shaping of the controlling idea. But the developing of the idea, or evolution of the spiritual image in the body, is not always, nor generally, instantaneous, but is progressive. The creation of the world instantaneously by the divine *fiat* is not now entertained by thinking men anywhere. It is a tenet that has passed out of science and philosophy. In fact, creation is not now an accomplished event. It is not a thing done, but one that is in the process of being done. The divine idea is not yet fully realized or actualized. The world is an unfinished picture. As the Platonists would say, it is in a state of *becoming*. The divine idea, the universal divine life, a mysterious power of order and arrangement, is at the very centre and heart of things, struggling to work itself out into a complete material expression. Universal nature is moved from within by the Universal Mind, of which our minds are a part.

In giving treatment to the body, which is our world, it is not so much our aim to impart life to it from without — though this can be done — as it is to aid the inner life, the real conscious self, and the true idea of our being in its birth into actuality or a material expression. The body, which is the external shell of our being, becomes fixed. The *tschamping, shampooing*, or *massage* may remove the hardness of the shell so that it can more readily take shape from the inward idea. *All motion, all progress, all development, is in the direction of the least resistance*, as James Hinton demonstrated. To remove obstructions, to break up the fixedness of the body, which is the characteristic of old age, to accelerate the process of excretion and disintegration, is to aid the process of the reformation of the body from within. In the germ of the animal body, as in the seed of the plant, there is the living idea of the future organism. And that idea forms the body after the pattern of itself. It is function (or idea) that creates its appropriate organ, and not the organ that makes the function. For instance, the heart is made to beat, and this action commences before its tissues are formed, even when it is only a fluid mass of protoplasmic jelly. So it is always the function, the idea, which creates its organic expression. Thus it is, and of necessity must be, in regard to the whole body.

If we will form the true idea of man, and apply it to ourselves, and hold it steadfastly in the mind, and *believe in its realization*, by one of the deepest and most certain laws of our nature, it will tend to recreate the body after the pattern of that mental type. Creation is a begetting, and nature means that which is born. It is the product of the divine idea expressing itself in our minds on the plane of sense. The renewal of the body by the creative power of the divine idea of man is the true *palingenesis* or regeneration. (Mat. xix: 28.)

It seems to be a divine law that all animal bodies are

renewed at least once a year. The crab and the lobster annually cast off the old shell, and a new one forms from within. The serpent sheds his skin, and this is the last step in the renewal of his body. Birds cast off their feathers, and this takes place by a cause or force that acts from within outward, and it is the last stage in the process of their renewal. The ox and the horse shed their hair in spring. The tree renews itself once a year, and a new one grows around the older ones, which in time decay, leaving the trunk hollow. Perennial plants die down to the root, where the infant plant-germ remains, and starts into life with youthful vigor in the spring. All these phenomena are illustrations of a general law of life that is called *rejuvenescence*. Man should move forward in this divine order. If we keep the mind ever young, the body can be left to take care of itself. Man, in health, casts off the external shell once a year, for there is nothing in the animal world that is not in man. He "renews his youth as the eagles"; but what the new body shall be depends on the character of the controlling idea and *fixed belief*, for the outer shell will shape itself into its material expression. As God creates the world by the Divine Idea, so we, in the same way, create our bodies, which are a microcosm, or world on a small scale. Every step in the disintegrating and renewing process is influenced by the governing idea, for the body exists, like everything else, in thought, and is what we think it to be. It is formed after the pattern of the image which we form of ourselves in the mind. If that is the divine and true idea of man, it will make our humanity divine, a thing of health, and harmony, and beauty, even in its ultimate manifestation in the body. If Jesus, as Swedenborg affirms, made his humanity divine even to its ultimates, it was effected by maintaining in thought, and steadfastly holding before his mind, the divine idea of man. Every new and higher conception which we form of the inward nature of man, and consequently of ourselves, by an undeviating law, tends to an outward bodily expression. It is the living germ, the *seed* of a new state, having a divine creative potency in it. A seed is one of the most marvellous things in nature. It is the embodiment of the *idea* of the future plant, containing in it a *conatus* or tendency to develop, under the proper conditions of soil and air, in the external world. So the kingdom of heaven, or the true spiritual condition of man, in its incipiency, is like a grain of mustard which a man plants in a field, and which afterward becomes unfolded into a tree, "bearing fruit and yielding seed after its kind." (Luke xiii : 19.) It is the business of the psychological physician to plant in the mind of the patient the *fruitful idea* of a better condition. He is like the husbandman that goes forth to sow, and often, from a single idea that finds lodgement in the interior mind, there is afterwards reaped an abundant harvest. (Mat. xiii : 3-9.) The kingdom of heaven, says Jesus, is also like leaven, which a woman took and hid in three measures of meal (the *sheah* was a peck and a half) until the whole was leavened. (Mat. xiii : 33.) If we can impart a new life to a patient, however little it may seem to be, it will propagate itself and multiply itself until it reduces the whole organism to its own nature. If our mode of thought is on a higher range, and our spiritual state above his, it will be easy to do this, on the principle that *water* runs down hill, or descends from a higher to a lower level. And whatever can be done at all by the psychological method, can be done easily and without labored effort. "The Father, who dwelleth in us, He doeth the works."

In the application of this important law to self-cure, we need to fix in our minds the change we know ought to be effected, or form the idea of the state to which we aspire, and in a measure we have already become what we desired to be. It is our right and privilege to *believe* this. As an artist said to Emerson, "A man cannot draw a tree without becoming in a certain sort a tree," so we cannot form the true idea of an animal without becoming in some degree that animal. In forming the true conception of a child, so that we could paint him as he is internally and externally, we become as a child, and think and feel as a child. The idea we form of an angel is not a mental picture or image of some one else, but is that of our true self. So we cannot form the true idea of ourselves, or of any mental state, without becoming in some good degree, the realization of it. To steadfastly *believe* this, and tenaciously adhere to it, is to experience the dawn of the state to which we aspire, and this by one of the deepest and most uniform laws in the whole world of mind.

CHAPTER XVI.

THE NATURE AND RIGHT USE OF THE WILL.

MUCH of the efficiency of the will is lost by our not understanding its true nature and the best method of its use. The highest conception of an act of the will is that it is an inward divine impulse towards a good end or aim. Paul affirms that it is God who worketh in us to will and to do of his good pleasure. (Phil. ii : 13.) The will is the innermost root of our life, and forever flows forth from the Divinity within us, the *theocentric* region of our spiritual being. This is also true of faith, which Paul also declares to be "the gift of God," or an emanation from Him. (Eph. ii: 8.) Hence, Jesus said to his disciples, "Have the faith of God." (Mark xi : 22, marginal reading.) Paul, in one of his Epistles, says that the life which he lived in the flesh, he lived by the faith of the Son of God (Gal. ii: 20), which is identical with the divine spirit of man and is in man. In another place he says, when it pleased God to reveal his Son *in me*, immediately I conferred not with flesh and blood, or no longer took counsel of the sensuous mind, as having a higher guidance within. (Gal. i : 16.) The imagination is also, when used in distinction from the fancy, a divine spiritual power, and as a mode of thought, is one of the most subtle and potent forces in the universe. The fancy belongs to the psychical or animal soul region, which is the region of illusion and sensuous fallacies. But thought is a manifestation of God. It is a power that arises perpetually out of the One Life, and is never sundered from it. (II Cor. iii: 5.) The will, the faith, the imagination, are the highest powers of the human mind, as they are an activity of the divine realm of our being — a stirring of deep divinity within us. If the end towards which these powers are directed is not a worthy one, we then, as it were, cut them loose from the Divinity in us, and they become only a spontaneous and perverted activity of the self-hood, or the selfish action of the animal soul. But there lies back of every virtuous and beneficent exercise of will, the life and tranquil omnipotence of the Deity. The Divine Mind is not sundered from our volitional activity, in our psychological effort to relieve pain and cure disease, any more than you can disconnect a ray of light from its central source. The will, and imagination, and faith are from God, and are God in man. Pythagoras taught his disciples that God is the Universal Mind diffused, as it were, through all things, and this mind, or intelligent life-principle, by virtue of its universal sameness, and that it is the inmost essence of all things, could be communicated from one object to another, and could be made to create all things by the individual will power of man. (*Isis Unveiled*, vol. 1, p. 131.) This is strong language, but there is a profound truth in it which comes from a philosophy older than the enlightened sage of Samos. Marvellous things, and to the world miraculous things, have been done by the *spirit*, which is the divine and miraculous man. The inseparable connection of a wise and good man with God, was a spiritual verity better understood by the older philosophers than by modern scientists, who seem to have wholly lost sight of it. It was taught as an esoteric doctrine in their occult science and wisdom-religion. Of modern philosophers, no one appears to have apprehended this sublime truth with greater clearness than Johann Godfried Fichte. He says of the will of man: "Every virtuous resolution (and we may say the same of every benevolent healing intention) influences the Omnipotent Will (or Life), if I may be allowed to use such an expression, not in consequence of a momentary approval, but of an everlasting law of his Being. With surprising clearness does the thought now come before my soul, which hitherto was surrounded with darkness, — the thought that my will, as such merely, and of itself, can have any results (or consequences)." (*Destination of Man*, p. 110.) In another place he says: "The will is the effective cause, the living principle of the *world of spirit*, as motion is of the world of sense, I stand between two opposite worlds; the one visible, in which the act alone avails, the other invisible and incomprehensible, acted on only by the will. I am an effective force in both these worlds. My will embraces both. The will is in itself a constituent part of the transcendental world. By my free determination I change and set in motion something in this transcendental world, and my energy gives birth to an effect that is new, permanent, and imperishable." (*Destination of Man*, p. 98.)

In using the will with a healing intention upon ourselves, or in making a psychological impression upon another, it first acts in and upon the Universal Life-Principle, and by reaction upon the mind of the patient or upon our own, as the case may be. And in this way we meet with no obstruction and tendency to contradict, as we often do when we approach the patient from without and verbally address him. A true healing influence goes forth from our inward spirit, but this is only an individual manifestation and personified expression of the One Spirit which is in full accord with the human spirit. In the psychological method of treating disease, it is a fundamental doctrine in which we must become immovably grounded, that a voluntary activity of mind is the only power and causal agent in the universe. Mind and will are the first principle of motion. On this subject Bishop Berkeley truly says: "It is plain philosophers amuse themselves in vain when they inquire for any natural, efficient cause distinct from a mind or spirit." (*Principles of Human Knowledge*, sec. 107.) In our effort to relieve suffering and cure disease by mental action, we may feel sure that we are acting from the realm of causation.

If we comprehend the principles laid down in what has been said above, as to the true nature of the will, and can appropriate them, we are prepared to receive instruction in the use of this spiritual power in its most intense and efficient form of action. It is to be observed that the will belongs to the Universal Life-Principle. It is not an active, but a passive or *reactive* potency. It is included in the department of the love or feeling, and in its highest form is the Chokma or Sophia of the Kabala, which in its correlations or descending degrees becomes the living force of the world. Thought or intelligence is the active or masculine potency, and the will the passive and feminine power. Thought speaks, and the will responds. In making a psychological impression, active thought or intelligence is the power, and the will of the patient is the responsive echo. The conception of the will as an active power, and a power capable of originating action of itself, has been a fundamental mistake in modern psychology, but one of which the ancient science of mind is free.

Thought is the highest active principle in the universe, and the will is an equally potent reactive force. But the most intense form of its action in a psychological, curative effort, upon ourselves or others, is not when it is put forth as a *command*, but as a positive *affirmation*. It does not say, "Be thou so and so," but rather, "You will be well," and in its highest expression, "You are well." It is to be remembered that the will is strengthened by faith, which is the ground of all reality, and the basis of all possibility. (Mark ix: 23; xi: 24.) The will is guided and qualified by the imagination. When it goes forth in an affirmation, the will, faith, and imagination are combined into a unity. Men instinctively use this form of will, without being able to give a reason for it. In the government of children in the school or family, when the child is directed to do a certain thing, and replies, "I will not," the parent or teacher says to him, "You *will* do it," rather than "I command you to do it." In military life we witness great numbers of men controlled by one despotic mind. The commanding general, in issuing his orders to his subordinates regulating the movements of a campaign or a battle, simply says to each of them, "You will do this or that," "You will move with your soldiers to yonder position," and it is done. In the first chapter of Genesis we have a sublime exhibition of the omnipotent, creative Thought, going forth as Will. It is not as in our common translation, "Let there be light, and there was light"; but, in the more eloquent simplicity of the original it is, "God said (or thought) Light *is;* and light was." It is only thought formulating itself in a positive affirmation. The more closely our finite minds imitate this divine form of expressing the will's potency, the more largely it will partake of God's omnipotence. This explains the reason of the influence of simple suggestion to one who is in the magnetic state. To say to a person, "You will be sick" or "You are sick," has an influence in making them so. To suggest to him "You are better" has more power to make him so than a thousand orders or commands. So to say to a wicked man that he is good, or will be so, has more reformative influence than all our commands or threats that we can utter. When the will goes forth in the form of a command, it throws the thing to be realized into the future; but when united with faith, and put forth as a positive affirmation, it views the thing to be done, the change to be effected, as a present reality, an accomplished fact. Hence Jesus said to the nobleman of Capernaum, "Thy son liveth"; and that very hour the fever left him. (Luke iv: 46–54.) To the invalid at the pool of Siloam he said: "Thou art made whole (or saved); sin no more, lest a worse thing come upon thee." (John v: 14.) To the woman who had a spirit of infirmity for eighteen years, calling her to him, he said, "Woman, thou art loosed from thine infirmity." (Luke xiii: 12.) And wherever in the language used by Jesus, the will seems to express itself in an imperative form, the real meaning is an affirmation, and the original is usually capable of that translation. When the leper of Capernaum said to him, "If thou *wilt*, thou canst make me clean," he replied "I will it; be thou clean"; that is, thou art clean — a form of expression which is based on the recognition of the fact, that in his inner being, his immortal self, he was free from the leprosy, and that it had an existence only in the body, which is no part of man. It is only an illusory veil which conceals the real man from view. The affirmation of Jesus, addressed to the inward man, was responded to by the man's will, and there was awakened in him a consciousness, a feeling of the truth of it. Thus the will exhibited its true nature, as a reactive principle, a responsive echo of thought. It is the *Verily*, the *Amen* of the New Testament; a word derived from the Hebrew *Amuna*, meaning truth. The rabbins believed it to possess a wonderful power. Its full significance is, when it is the response to an affirmation, "That is truth, and I believe it."

It is proper to remark, in closing, that a strong will-force makes no more exertion in a silent curative effort, directed to ourselves or others, than the mind makes in believing and affirming that two and two are four. All labored effort, all strain, all struggling is not will, but the lack of it. We should recognize the fact, the eternal verity, that the thing to be done, as the cure of a malady, or anything that may be viewed as the "good pleasure" of God, is from this very fact, in an effort to *become* an actuality. And the attitude of the will towards it is properly expressed by the word *fiat*, which means "let it be done or become." "If we ask anything according to his will, we know that he heareth us."

(I John v: 14.) The thing to be done, the object to be effected is like a spiral spring which is pressed down by a weight laid upon it. Yet there is a tendency in it to rise, and it will do so, and assume its cone-like form as soon as the obstruction is removed. We are potentially already what we ideally aspire to and long for, and will some time become so actually. For an idea that has life in it will assert itself.

All the volition that is necessary in making a psychological impression upon a patient is that of a *wish* or benevolent desire, expressing itself in an affirmation. This is the radical meaning of the word volition, from the Latin *volo*, to wish. This adds to the *thought* — the mere intellectual conception — an element of life-force. The influence of desire or emotion is to give intensity to the thought, to render it more vivid, or living, as the word means. Desire alone is powerless; and thought alone is lifeless and inefficient. They must be combined into a harmonious unity. In the language of the Hermetic philosophy, they must be made into a cross, in which the upright line is the intellect, and the horizontal or base line is the love or the emotional nature. This makes a living force, what Swedenborg calls the power of truth from good. It may be represented by the light of winter which is in excess of heat, and the life of the world is then dormant. In spring, the light, which answers to the truth, is equally combined with heat, which corresponds to love, and everything starts into life. In every genuine act of faith there is a union of thought and emotion, or an intellectual conception and a feeling that it is true. This is what makes it the " word of power."

It is taught in one of the sacred books of the Hindus, the Atharva-Veda, *that the exercise of such will-power is the highest form of prayer*, and it is instantaneously answered. For we realize in proportion to the intensity of our desire and the strength of our faith freed from all doubt. For desire is the incipiency of the thing or state desired, and faith is its full fruition.

CHAPTER XVII.

THE UNIVERSAL LIFE-PRINCIPLE, AND ITS OCCULT PROPERTIES AND USES.

WE see everywhere in nature the indications of a universal and intelligent force which governs the world. We behold, in whatever way we look,

> "The tokens of a central force,
> Whose circles, in their widening course,
> O'erlap and move the universe."

It is the common bond and life of nature, and exhibits a *conatus* to repair the hurts of every living thing, — of plants and animals, from the mushroom to the sovereign of an empire. It is the office of the physician to influence, direct, and control the universal principle of life, to come to its aid in its curative endeavor, and to intensify its action and diminish or increase its *quantum*. Says Lord Lytton, who, if not an adept, was deeply versed in the arcane philosophy of the East, "To all animate bodies there must be one principle in common, — the vital principle itself. What if there be one certain means of recruiting this principle? And what if that secret can be discovered?" (*A Strange Story*, p. 104.) Van Helmont, to whom science owes a debt of gratitude the world has never paid, was the discoverer of hydrogen *gas*, and he affirms that the life-principle is of the nature of a gas, a word which etymologically signifies *spirit*, like the German *geist*. In this sense, that of a universally diffused and omnipresent and omniactive *substance* of life, the assertion of Van Helmont was made, and only in this sense can it be accepted. It is stored up in exhaustless and overflowing abundance in the bosom of nature. It cannot be destroyed, or increased, or diminished. It cannot be created or annihilated. It is one and indivisible, and can be controlled in its lower degrees of manifestation by the intelligent will of man, which is the highest form of its development and expression. It is identical with what is called magnetism, which is a word of Persian origin, and signifies the "wisdom-principle." The life-principle is in itself without quality, and is a blind force obedient to a controlling influence. It is submissive to the will of the spiritual man, and servilely obeys it. It acts according to the direction given to it by our imagination, and tends to realize our idea, as the hand and brush of the painter follow the image which they copy from his mind. Of this universal life-principle Madam Blavatsky observes: "We breathe and imbibe it into our organic system with every mouthful of fresh air. Our organism is full of it from the instant of our birth, but it becomes potential only under the influx of *will* and *spirit*." (*Isis Unveiled*, vol. i., p. 616.) This invisible and ubiquitous life-principle, the *anima mundi* of Plato, and the magnetic agent, has occult properties and potencies in it that few know anything about. It obeys our thoughts and takes quality from them. It answers to the human voice, and yields to the impulse of our will, and even understands the meaning of *traced signs* and motions of the hand, especially if they are correspondences. However incredible this may seem, it is nevertheless true, as Baron Du Potet, the prince of modern magnetists, affirms. But why should it not be so, since the rational soul of man, the immortal *psyche*, is only the highest expression of the universal soul or the intelligent life-principle in nature? And when the soul is closely united to this universal force it possesses, if we only but knew it, a marvellous power. It is then, as it were, the general in command of the universal living energy to direct it to the accomplishment of a desired result. Life is everywhere. A desire of recovery is a search after life, and this, as Emerson says of power, is an element with which the world is so saturated — there being no chink or crevice in which it is not lodged — that no honest seeking need go unrewarded. All matter is animated and acted upon by invisible agencies, of which heat and light are the most apparent. But these are only expressions on the plane of sense of the invisible and imponderable life-principle. Heat in its spiritual essence is a feeling, and light is truth.

> "This conscious life, is it the same
> Which thrills the universal frame,
> Whereby the caverned crystal shoots,
> And mounts the sap from forest roots,
> Whereby the exiled wood-bird tells
> When spring makes green her native dells?
> How feels the stone the pang of birth
> Which brings its sparkling prism forth?
> The forest tree the throb which gives
> The life-blood to its new-born leaves?"
>
> (*Whittier.*)

In his "Coming Race," a work which contains many hints respecting the Oriental occult science, Lord Lytton denominates the universal life-principle and primal force, which the Hindu adepts call the *akasa*, by the unusual name of *vril*, and says that in *vril* his underground people thought that "they had arrived at the unity in natural energetic agencies." Like the *akasa* of the Hindu transcendental science, it is a sort of "atmospheric magnetism," and controllable by the imagination and will of man. It is the "*occult air*" of the Kabalists, and is called by the Jewish prophets "the breath of God" and "the breath of life." Its nature, hidden properties, the laws of its action, and how to control it, was undoubtedly a part of the esoteric teaching in the prophetic schools. It is clearly mentioned in the celebrated vision of the dry bones in Ezekiel, "Come from the fou winds, O breath, and breathe upon these slain, and they shall live." (Ezek. xxxvii: 9.) Is it true that this subtle and universal element of life will come at our call, and can we give it quality and modify its action? If so, it is the most important thing that medical philosophy can teach. Of the occult philosopher Haroun of Aleppo, Lord Lytton says: "He had discovered the great principle of animal life, which had hitherto baffled the subtlest anatomist, and provided only that the great organs were not irreparably destroyed, there was no disease that he could not cure, no decrepitude to which he could not restore vigor; yet his science was based on the same theory as that espoused by the best professional practitioners of medicine, viz., that the true art of healing is to assist nature to throw off the disease, — to summon, as it were, the whole system to eject the enemy that had fastened on a part. And thus his processes, though occasionally varying in the means employed, all combined in this, viz., the reinvigorating and recruiting of the principle of life." (*A Strange Story*, p. 186.)

"The universal substance," says Eliphas Levi, "*with its double motion* (its active and reactive properties), is the great arcanum of being." This is profoundly true. This preëxistent and invisible essence of things which we call *life*, this elemental and universal substance, is often latent in nature, and is without form or quality in itself, but receives quality from our imagination or thought, just as water takes form from the glass vessel that contains it. We see illustrations of this in the life of men. If a person swallows a few drops of water, or a pill made of bread crumbs, *thinking* it a cathartic medicine, it will give to it that quality, and it will quicken the peristaltic movement of the intestinal canal. Thought has power to alter the nature of things so as to radically change their quality. This is implied in the promise of Jesus, that, if we believe, or have faith, to drink any deadly thing will not harm us. Thus Paul overcame the otherwise fatal bite and poison of the viper. Jesus also says, "Be it unto thee according to thy faith"; but faith is only a mode of thought. The passive life-principle of the human body and of all things is as sensitive to the influence of thought and imagination as the mercury in the bulb of the thermometer or barometer is to atmospheric changes. This universal life-principle and primordial substance has an affinity for our inward character, as some one has said, and is *en rapport* with the purposes which we wish to effect by it, — as the relief of pain and the cure of disease. Our minds and wills can give quality to it; and by the projectile power of the mind, and by a thought-impulse, a current or tendency of it can be determined upon the body of another, to recruit and augment his vital energy. By certain movements of the hands, which are but the expression of our thoughts, we can cause it to accumulate in the brain, and the whole physical organism or any part of it, and its invigorating effects will sometimes border on the marvellous. The reinforcing the vital power of the whole system is the shortest and most direct way of curing any diseased part. The air and the water contain all the invisible essences of things, that from which all plants and minerals arise, and of which they are, so to speak, only condensations, or *precipitations*, so that they become manifest to our crude senses. We see granite rock floating in the air in the form of dust. But there is an invisible, imponderable *dust*, or primal stuff, or substance, — the mysterious *clay* of the first chapter of Genesis, — out of which dust the body of man was and is formed, and to which it returns. These spiritual virtues and living principles of things are controllable by the will, faith, and imagination of man, and can, with any quality our thought may give them, be determined upon the body or any of its organs. They can also be infused into any inert substances, as milk-sugar, or water, or even paper, and they become invested with the peculiar properties of any herb or drug. But all this lies within the unexplored domain of the occult science of medicine. In an old work by a Scotch physician by the name of Maxwell, entitled "Medicina Magnetica," and published at Frankfort in 1679, it is said: "That which men call the world spirit (the welt-geist of the German, the *anima mundi* of the Platonic philosophy) is a *life*, as fire, spiritual, fleet, subtle, and ethereal as light itself. It is a life-spirit everywhere, and everywhere the same; and this is the common bond of all quarters of the earth, and lives through and in all.

"If thou canst avail thyself of this spirit and accumulate it in particular bodies, thou wilt receive no trifling benefit from it, for therein consists all the mystery of magic (or magnetism). This spirit is found in nature free from all fetters; and he who understands how to unite it to a harmonizing body possesses a treasure which exceeds all riches."

"*He who knows how to operate on men by this spirit can heal, and this at any distance he pleases.*" (*Ennemoser's History of Magic*, Vol. II., p. 258.) This brief extract contains the key to the mystery of healing by magnetism, and by mental forces and agencies. The true magnetic healer has learned the nature and properties of the universal divine life-principle, and how to influence its action. It is an exalted science in its higher applications, and will be rescued from its present degradation, and restored to its ancient dignity as the science of sciences. It was once called magic, a word which signifies wisdom, for it was a true spiritual philosophy, founded upon immutable and eternal principles, and was practised by many of the noblest and divinest men the world ever saw.

CHAPTER XVIII.

THE UNIVERSAL ETHER OF SCIENCE, AND THE ÆTHER OF THE HERMETIC PHILOSOPHY.

MAGNETISM, as the universal life-principle, and that by which God is present and acts in nature, is in a perpetual effort to ultimate or actualize the divine idea of things in material forms. This effort we believe can be aided, and its operation greatly accelerated, by the intelligent will and imagination of man. When I think that a patient is well, or is getting well, — and this is true, as has been shown before, of his immortal *self* or spiritual entity, — the thought by an occult law takes form in an idea, in the Logos or Divine Truth, as Swedenborg would call it, which is a spiritual and *living* substance. But this idea will take a more external shape in the universal soul-life of nature, the primal substance or cosmic matter. It then becomes a real creation, an ideal entity, a thing of the *unseen world*. But the soul of the patient is a part of the soul of the world and not disconnected from it; and on his soul the ideal picture may be photographed, and it will still tend outward by a force proportioned to the intensity of the original thought and vividness of the idea, until it translates itself into a full bodily expression, or creates the physical organism into its own image. "An idea," says Plutarch, "is a being (or thing) incorporeal, which has no subsistence by itself, but gives figure and form unto shapeless matter, and becomes the cause of its manifestation." (*De Placitio Philosophorum.*) The cosmic matter, the primal stuff of which all things are made (and which is recognized in science as the universal æther), and which is the same everywhere and in all things in the universe, *is of itself without form or quality. It is the original chaos. It only receives form and quality from ideas which are in mind only.* Hence it is that mind shapes matter, and gives it all its properties. This universally diffused principle, the great magnetic agent, and which Sir Isaac Newton called the *divine sensorium* (for it is really the seat of all sensation), is the *anima mundi*, the soul of the world. The animal soul of man is an individualized expression of it, and through it we are connected in sympathy with all other souls, and all the objects of nature, even to the stars and all the heavenly bodies. Newton says of it in his "Fundamental Principles of Natural Philosophy" : "Here the question is of a very subtle spirit, which penetrates through all, even the hardest bodies, and which is concealed in their substance. Through the strength and activity of this spirit (or immaterial substance) bodies attract each other, and adhere together when brought into contact. Through it electrical bodies operate at the remotest distance, as well as near at hand, attracting and repelling (he might have said that in it and by it distance is annihilated, and all objects touch each other) ; through this spirit (or intelligent, *im*-material substance), light also flows and is refracted and reflected, and warms bodies. *All senses are excited by this spirit*, and through it the animals move their limbs. But these things cannot be explained in few words, and we have not yet sufficient experience to determine fully the laws by which this universal spirit operates." Thus far and no farther can modern science go. But the Archaic or Hermetic philosophy gives to the universal *æther* certain occult metaphysical properties, with which it was familiar, but of which our modern materialistic science is totally ignorant. The word is from αἴθω (*aitho*), to burn, to shine. This æther, according to Pythagoras, Empedocles, Plato, Hyppasus, Heraclitus, Hippocrates, and all the oldest philosophers, was viewed as a divine, luminous principle or substance, which permeates, and at the same time *contains* all things in it. It was called by the Hermetic philosophers the *astral light*, which signifies not star-light, as the word would seem to indicate, but the feminine wisdom-principle, it being from the same root as Astarte and Ashtaroth. It is a spiritual fire that does not burn. In the treatise on the Nature of the Gods (Lib. ii., c. 36), Cicero says: *Aërem amplectatur immensus æther, qui constat, exaltissimis ignibus*, the immensurable æther, which consists of the most subtle and exalted fire or flame, embraces the air. Also Apuleius ("De Mundo") says: *Cœlum ipsum stellasque colligens, omnisque siderum compago, æther vocatur, non ut quidem putant quod ignitus sit et incensus, sed quod cursibus rapidis semper rotatur*. The æther is that in which all things exist when we get round to their immaterial side. All life is compared to a flame, and the soul is poetically, but truly said to be a vital spark of heavenly fire. All growing things assume the flame form, as leaves and grasses. The æther is the unparticled substance, of which all things are made, and to which they return. The fire of which John the Baptist speaks, the baptismal flame, is identical with the Holy Spirit, and is the universal æther of occult philosophy; for it was not viewed as material in the common acceptation of the term. In the Book of Hermes, called Pimander, which signifies the Divine Thought, it is said: "The light is I. I am the *nous* or intelligence, and I am thy god, and I am far older than the human principle which escapes from the shadow. I am the germ of thought, the resplendent Word, the Son of God. Think that what thus sees and hears in thee, is the *Verbum* of the Master, it is the Thought which is God the Father. The celestial ocean, the *æther*, which flows from *east to west*, is the Breath of the Father, the life-giving principle, the Holy Ghost."

The universal æther, according to the authors of that remarkable book, the "Unseen Universe," is the repository of the *spiritual images* of all living things, and even human thoughts. All things that ever were, that are, or ever will be, all that was ever said or written, thought and felt, leaves its record upon this imperishable tablet of the unseen world; and the truly spiritual man, by using the vision of his own spirit, may read it there, and know all that has been known or can be known; for it still exists in the universal principle, which is the Apocalyptic "book of life," and the mysterious "tree of knowledge" of Genesis, and the memory of God.

It is one of the fundamental ideas of the work mentioned above, that "thought affects the matter (or substance) of another world simultaneously with this," and the missing link connecting mind and matter is thus found, and the great law of continuity is maintained. A blow on the body of another affects not merely the external shell, but goes deeper, and wounds and scars the primitive matter of the body. So a treatment given to another in kindness and a desire to heal, affects the inner man, and through that tends to form the external body into the image of health and divine harmony.

A thought impulse can affect and set in motion the universal *æther*, the life-principle. It can create a current in the *astral light*, the *welt-geist* of the German, and give it quality, and direct it to a person near at hand, or send it as a sanative influence to any distance. Few persons know of the marvellous power that lies latent and slumbering in human nature; and it is well it is so.

Our thoughts and feelings are not the evanescent things they are supposed to be, but they record themselves on this unseen tablet, and create a current, or, as it were, an eddying sphere, in the universal æther or life. The prevailing mode of thinking and predominant feelings of an age or community create a current or tendency in the world's life that bears us on with it, and it is hard to row against the stream. This is what is called in the teaching of Jesus *the world*, which is viewed as the antagonist of the spiritual life. "Ye are not of the world, but I have chosen you out of the world," by which is not meant the earth, but the general current of thought and feeling in the age and country where we live. To the spiritual eye most souls are seen floating in it like the dead and withered leaves of autumn upon the surface of a swollen and muddy stream. To take a patient and lift him out of this current of established beliefs and confirmed illusions, is the Herculean task before the true physician. When one is sick in any degree, the general current of the world's life leads him to think that he must *take* something, or do something. There is only one way in which we can not only *stem* this flood, but rise entirely out of it into a higher stratum of thought and feeling, and that is through the power of an intelligent faith. "This is the victory that overcometh the world, even your faith." (I John iv: 4.) "And to him that overcometh, will I give to eat of the tree of life which is in the Paradise of God." (Rev. ii: 7.) This is purely Kabalistic, but full of meaning to him who has the key to it. The garden of God, according to the old science of correspondence, signifies spiritual wisdom and its delights. "The tree of life" is the Kabalistic Adam Kadmon, the primal and universal spiritual man, the true *maximus homo*, or greatest man, of the Scandinavian seer. To eat of this tree is to come into direct communication with the central fountain of all manifested life, that from which all existence springs, and to which it seeks to return. This is the elixir of life, "the spiritual essence of silver" of the Alchemists and Hermetic philosophers. The tree of life of the Kabala was represented with its roots upwards and branches downwards. So we need to be taken up from our present inverted condition,—the illusory life of sense,—and transplanted into the garden of God, and planted with the spiritual root of our being upward, and we shall bear fruit downward. We shall receive influx from above, and no longer from beneath, from the mephitic vapors of the Stygian lake. Then we reach the secret of a long life in that tranquillity of mind which results from a life above the *world*, or that sphere or current of mental disorder that constitutes the life of men in general. It is on this plane alone that disease (which in its essence is discontent, dissatisfaction) can exist. On the spiritual plane we look down upon it, like earthly fogs seen from the summit of a mountain.

In closing this lesson I would remark that things become necessary to the sustenance or maintenance of life in proportion as they become more and more subtle and interior.

1. We have the mineral and earthy elements in our food. A due proportion of these is essential to the preservation of the integrity of the corporeal structure.

2. Water, which is an element less gross than minerals, and we can live longer without food than we can without water.

3. The air, which is more subtle than the aqueous element and a thousand times more necessary to life.

4. Lastly, the universal æther, the principle of life itself, and the universal magnetic agent.

We must caution the reader against taking a too material conception of this subtle principle, as is done by modern science, but was not done in the ancient Hermetic philosophy. This is the "one thing needful," a designation applied to it in the old spiritual science, and often recurring in the writings of the Alchemists of all ages, and also employed by Jesus in his conversation with Martha. (Luke x: 38-42.) It is that *rema* or emanation from God, from which man lives more than from bread. (Luke iv: 4.)

CHAPTER XIX.

THE MOTHER PRINCIPLE OF THINGS, AND ITS USE IN SELF-HEALING.

The universal life-principle in its latent state is the primal matter and cosmic substance, and fills all space, and connects all worlds. It pervades and *contains* the air, as the air contains the water, and the water the earth. We inhale it with every breath, and in it we live, and move, and have our being. But it is "without form and void" of quality. It is pure *existence*, and to it properties and qualities are given by thought alone. To it any quality can be given by the imagination as we breathe it in. It is the mother principle, the feminine creative potency, the passive power in nature, and is co-eternal with spirit, of which it is the correlative opposite. It is an interesting fact that the word *mother* and *matter* are nearly identical in most of the languages of the world. In Latin we have *mater* and *materia*, the matter, stuff, or material of which anything is made. In Italian, *madre* signifies mother, cause, origin, root, spring, and mould for castings. In the latter sense, the mother principle is the universal matrix. In Spanish we have *madre*, mother, and *materia*, matter. In Portuguese, *madre* means mother and the mould for castings. Even in the Irish, *mathair* means mother and also matter. This primal matter is the mother principle, or feminine passive ray, emanating from the "Unknown." It is the universal mould in which all ideas take shape. It is represented in the Jewish cosmogony by Eve (or Heva), "the mother of all living things," the very name signifying completeness and fulness of life. The feminine principle of things is not absolutely passive, but its characteristic is *reaction*. The quality which we impress by our thought upon this universal life-principle, it takes, and it is reflected back with it in the respiration. The sun shines by its own light, and the feminine moon reflects. There is an *occult air*, immaterial and imperceptible to any of the gross external senses, but most vitally real, for things increase in reality as they come nearer to the central point of existence. "This air," says the Kabala, "is the most occult (*occultissimus*) attribute of the Deity." It is identical with the *akasa* of the Hindu philosophy. In its latent state it is the universal æther, the air of immensity, "an unburning vivific flame." It is the Shekinah of the Hebrew Scriptures, and the Holy Spirit of the New Testament as a feminine life-principle. The Shekinah is that subtle light, or divine luminous substance, or visible glory, which was a symbol and vehicle of the divine presence. It was the sacred fire of the Persians, and the Astral light of the Rosicrucians. This primal, *everywhere-present* principle, or immaterial substance, is the universal *matrix* in which the ideas of the intellect take form and become to our minds and senses visible entities. In the Hindu theosophy, the grandest system of metaphysics the world has ever seen, it is called Nari and Mariāma, the universal mother. It was symbolized by the Lotus; and Brahm, the active masculine potency seated on the Lotus floating on the water creates the world. In the Egyptian philosophy it was called Isis, and the attributes and names given to it. the Roman Catholic system has borrowed and given to Mary, which name means the sea as a feminine principle. In the Archaic wisdom-religion this universal principle was denominated the mother-soul of the universe and the astral virgin, which waits to be fertilized or impregnated by the intellect or male potency. It was called pure essence, the mother of the five virtues, elements, or potencies: in other words, the primal force from which all the forces of nature spring. She was also called wise mother, mirror of *justice*, or real truth, as all the knowledge of the world in every age is recorded in it as in a sealed book. It was also the symbol and the repository of the occult science of the ancient sages, and represented by the ark. Hence Isis was veiled, to signify that this spiritual science and mystic wisdom was concealed from the world at large. The unveiling of Isis was the revelation of the hidden truths of the arcane philosophy. Both Nari and Isis were called *womb* of gold, *sistrum* of gold, and virgin queen of heaven — *cœlum*, which is from the Greek *koilia*, the belly, the womb of the universe, signified by the blue vault with its mysterious depths, the blue ray being the feminine color. She was the mother-soul of all beings and things. It is the source of all celestial light, the morning star of the Apocalypse (Rev. ii: 28), the Syrian Astarte, the Jewish Astaroth, and the astral light of the Kabala.

Creation, as we have said before, and here repeat, is a begetting; that is, it is the union of the male principle — pure spirit, the *nous* of Plato, the primal light — with the feminine principle, the Sophia, the *prima materia*, the pure cosmic immaterial substance. The first is represented by the upright line or descending ray (|), and the latter, by the horizontal or base line (—), and the union of the two forms the cross (+), one of the oldest and most expressive of religious symbols. "All that is created," says the Kabala, "by the Ancient of the Ancients, can live and exist only by a male and a female" (principle). Thought and feeling, idea and sensation, combine to make a thing, a concrete reality.

The most ancient name of the Deity, the Mystic designation of God, and found in all the Archaic esoteric religious philosophies, expresses this truth. It was IAO, pronounced by the Jews — if uttered at all — Yaho, and by the Samaritans, Yava. Its significance was kept absolutely occult, and deeply veiled from the multitude. It is composed of the masculine upright line (|) as the one or unity, and the feminine, ought (0) or cypher. The two in combination make the number ten (10), which, in its symbolic esoteric sense, means all, and fulness, completeness, the Alpha and the Omega, the first and the last, and all between the extremes.

With the *H* or *Ah*, the *aspirate* or *breathing*, which mystically signifies breath, soul, life, coming between the masculine upright and the representative of the feminine passive or *reactive* principle, the oval, egg-shaped ought, the Sanscrit Siphron, it teaches that all things that live and exist, consciously and unconsciously, are generated by the conjunction of these two principles. And the most ancient name of God, IAO, means that He is the All, that we and all other creatures are included in his Being, and that "he giveth life, and *breath*, and all things." The egg, the oval, the cypher, is the representative of the feminine universal life-principle and creative potency, and it was a tenet of the occult philosophy, that all things are produced from an egg. But the cypher by itself stands for nothing; in union with the one (pure spirit) it means all things. In the Creation, the Divine Spirit *brooded over* the "face of the waters." As all the emotions and interior feelings are expressed in the face, it came to signify the inmost pure essence of things. Over this the Spirit brooded and gave it form and quality. But man, in his complete being, reaches from the last (matter) to the first (spirit), from earth to the highest heaven. Our spirits can imitate the creative act of the Elohim. Thought, which is a movement of the Divine Spirit in man, and springs out of the unknown depths of the Godhead, can act on this universal passive principle, and in it, it will take form in an idea, which is a living *thing*, an actual creation or thing begotten. This universal mother principle is that through which thought is made effective.

Celestial wisdom, the Divine Sophia, the second emanation of the Kabala, by a law of correlation or correspondence, in its descent downward, or its passing outward from the living Point (the Centre which is everywhere, of a circle which is nowhere) becomes the reactive mother principle of nature, the cosmic matter, or immaterial substance, the chaos, the *hyle* of Plato and the Greeks, the *prima materia*. It is the Sakti of the Buddhists, the sacred presence, the veil of God, the instrument or agent of the active power and creative energy of gods and men. It is the *vehan* or vehicle or medium of communication between one mind and another, and through which a psychological impression can be made, and ideas communicated by psychological telegraphy far and near. It is the *messenger dove*, the carrier pigeon of the spirit, the invisible and everywhere present, and divinely sensitive silver wire through which a thought impulse may be transmitted over continents and across oceans. It is that by which God is present in the world, and through which one spirit may be present to another spirit a thousand miles away, for in it, distance ceases to be, and all objects may touch and communicate. It is also the universal principle of *sensation*, that in which all sensation and perception exist, and *through which a sensation may be transmitted any distance*. It is the universal eye, the all hearing ear, and the omnipresent sense of feeling. It is the medium of sympathy, or psychometry, or that through which our states affect others, and our feelings become infectious. *All this, and much more*, is true of it.

This knowledge was kept for ages absolutely occult, and has, for wise reasons, been concealed from the rabble from the foundation of the world. It was taught by "the wise men" to the elected few, but under allegorical forms of expression was hidden from the unthinking multitudes, to whom it was not given to know the mysteries of the kingdom of God, and it is fully known only to a chosen few to-day. It still belongs to that wisdom which Paul spoke only among the perfect. But the time is at hand when it may be proper to unloose the seven seals, and in *some degree* open the mystic scroll that is written within and on the backside (Rev. 7:1). And the knowledge of this arcane philosophy will invest the soul of man with greatly enlarged powers of doing good, and of " working the works of God." In the possession of this spiritual science, magnetism becomes the wisdom-lore of the ancient sages, — the knowledge of spiritual things, and their relation to natural things. Religion becomes the recognition of the Father and Mother sides of the Divine Being, — an *androgyne* Deity, the divine character rounded out into full-orbed completeness, and not a one-sided, stern, inflexible, masculine power and justice. And heaven itself, with its angelic hosts, is moved up from the immense remoteness, where the theology of materialism has placed it, into actual *contact* with men's souls.

In our Western theology, the masculine side of the divine nature has been pushed into extreme prominence, to the exclusion of the feminine side. In the Hindu system the reverse of this is true, and Mozoomdar boldly affirms, " We believe in a Mother God." It is an interesting fact that among them the Supreme Divine Essence, the *Aditi* (from *a*, not, and *diti*, bounded), is feminine, as the form of the Sanscrit word indicates. Hence, to the Hindu mind, the Absolute Divinity is passive and *responsive*, which ought to lay a firm foundation for faith in prayer. This is only another way of saying, " God is love," as love is the feminine side of human nature, and true love is an irrepressible inclination and impulse to give. In Swedenborg's " Science of Correspondence," the Father signifies the Divine Love, by which conception the sterner features of the Masculine Divinity of the popular theology are softened into motherhood, and the God we adore becomes tenderly responsive to our supplications, as the maternal instinct with loving haste flies to the rescue of her waiting child. In the Roman Catholic Religion, Mary is worshipped as a representative of the Universal Mother, and thus they unconsciously appeal to the Mother nature of God, and have accomplished the use of keeping alive in the Western mind this idea. Among them, Mary is the healer, and thus they teach without knowing it a great truth. There is in God, in the Christ, in Jesus, and in every holy and truly spiritual being, a masculine and feminine element. The perfect harmony and balancing of these is the highest condition of man. But it is the feminine element that binds up the hurts of every living thing. Nari, Isis, and Mary represent the maternal side of the Divine Being, and the feminine divine life-principle in nature. The original trinity was not that of Father, Son, and Holy Ghost, but was expressed by the relations of Father, Mother, and Son. This is given us in the "Timæus" of Plato, but came from the much older philosophy of India. Each discrete degree of the human mind is dual; that is, it is constituted of intellect, and sensibility or feeling, a masculine and feminine element in union. So in the Divine Mind and all its manifestations and incarnations. Suppose, in the Christian theology, we should view the Holy Spirit as the universal Mother element, it would at first be suspected of heresy, but nevertheless would express an eternal truth. But such is the fixedness of religious opinions, that the bare mention of the divine motherhood *in* God is deemed improper, and subjects one to the charge of being "a setter forth of strange gods." But everything in nature is dual. The air we breathe is a union of two gases, oxygen and nitrogen, — a positive and masculine, and a negative or feminine element. So water is a combination of oxygen and hydrogen. Minerals and earths follow the same law. All the salts of chemistry — and their name is legion — are a union of an acid and an alkali. Marble is carbonic acid and lime, and is carbonate of lime.

THE PRIMITIVE MIND-CURE. 155

The maternal element in God and nature is manifested in the tender, protecting, nursing, and healing care of the maternal parent among animals for her young. Jesus refers us to the hen as an illustration. Take these qualities and attributes exhibited everywhere in nature in the ineffable tenderness of motherhood, and project the idea upon the plane of the infinite, and you have our conception of the universal divine life-principle. We may call it Eve, or Mary, or the Holy Spirit, but must not separate it from God. We may always trust in it to cure our maladies of body and mind, and can pray to this side of the divine character. It furnishes a secure standing ground for an assured faith, and will until "mothers cease their own to cherish." When we fully grasp the idea, it will ever say to us in the words of Jesus, "Be not afraid; only believe." (Mark v : 36.)

The union of intellect and feeling, the masculine and feminine elements, to constitute a world, a thing, a perfected and complete human entity, is the symbolic significance of the cross, which expresses one of the grandest, most far-reaching and all-comprehensive truths in the whole realm of mind. Thus we rescue the sacred cross from its degradation in the modern theology, and restore it to its ancient and true meaning, and its saving, healing power. It is said that Constantine, the Roman emperor, had a vision of a cross in the heavens, on which was inscribed the letters I. H. S. *vince*. That meant, and still means, *In hoc signo, vince*, in what this sign signifies, conquer; for the truth, sublime in its simplicity, symbolized by the cross, is of the widest practical importance in the system of mental cure. The union of intellectual thought with feeling or emotion generates power. The omnipotence of God is the conjunction of infinite wisdom and infinite love. The union of the Divine Intellect and the Divine Love is Life, and all conscious and unconscious life is the result of that conjunction, a truth we have aimed to keep before the mind of the reader of these lessons. Hence the cross is the Kabalistic "tree of life." The highest psychological power is attained when we *feel* the truth we *know* and express. When the principle of spiritual intelligence in us is conjoined with its correlative emotion, it becomes a supreme saving and healing power. Intelligence alone, unvivified by love, is cold and dead, and has no more animating power than moonbeams reflected from polar ice. The healing power of Jesus was the result of the union of a divine intelligence with a pure, unselfish love, and his very *name* signifies and represents the saving principle that is the product of that union, as we shall have occasion to illustrate hereafter.

CHAPTER XX.

THE KABALISTIC AND MESSIANIC METHOD OF HEALING, AND THE ONE PRACTISED BY JESUS THE CHRIST.

THAT the cures wrought by Jesus were effected by the application of certain fixed principles, which, when properly formulated, constitute an intelligible transcendental mode or science of cure, there can be little doubt. His practical metaphysics are not an impenetrable and incommunicable secret. The knowledge of its leading principles is attainable by the spiritually enlightened mind to-day, and that knowledge will invest us with the power to do the works that he did. It was the practical application of the Messianic method of cure, described in symbolic language in the Kabala. In the Sohar, or Book of Light, of Rabbi Simon Ben Jochai, it is said: " In the garden of Eden (which was in the lower region of the spiritual world, corresponding to the soul region in man) there is one palace which is called the palace of the sick. The Messiah goes into this palace and invokes all the sufferings, and pains, and afflictions of Israel *to come upon him, and they all come upon him.* Now if he did not remove them thus, and take them upon himself, no man could endure the sufferings of Israel, due as a punishment for transgressing the Law: as it is written, ' Surely he hath borne our griefs and carried our sorrows.'" (Isa. lii: 4.) (See Ginsburg's *Kabala*.) This remarkable passage from the Kabala gives no foundation for the current doctrine of vicarious atonement, which was wholly foreign to the Jewish mind, but gives the key to a method of healing practised by Jesus, and perhaps also by the mystic Pythagorean sect of the Jews called Essenes, and also in Egypt Therapeutæ or Healers, to which sect Jesus himself unquestionably belonged. Through the *sympathetic* or *psychometric sense*, which may be defined as the susceptibility of being affected by the states of others, and which detects with unerring accuracy the mental condition of the patient, which is the spiritual cause of his disease, we take it on ourselves, at least so far as to have a clear conception of it. This wonderful " soul-measuring " power is represented by the golden reed in the hand of the apocalyptic angel, by which he took the measure of man, that is, detected the quality of a person. By it we take up into ourselves the condition of the patient, not to permanently carry it, but temporarily take it up intellectually and in *idea*, in order to loosen its hold upon him and to remove it from him. It is as if we should find a man by the wayside prostrate on the ground, with a rock which has fallen upon him holding him down. We lift the rock from him, not in order to carry it ourselves, but only to remove it from him. So it is said of Jesus that he fulfilled the saying of the Book of the prophet Isaiah, " Himself took up (or assumed to himself) our infirmities, and bore away (or removed) our diseases." (Mat. viii : 17.) We turn toward the patient the psychometric or " soul-measuring " sense, or the receptive side of human nature, which may become acutely developed in us, in order to receive into our minds the *idea*, the mental image, the *living psychic germ* of the disease. This is the spiritual side, the immaterial counterpart of the malady. This we take up, as it were, into ourselves, not sensationally only a slight degree, but rather intellectually, in order that as a cause of the disease, it may be *remitted* or borne away from the patient. Space is filled with the psychic germs or embryos of things. These are identical with the *atoms* of Democritus. The general current of the world-life is crowded with the soul-germs of disease, which in their essence are morbid ideas and fallacious beliefs. These are the latent causes, a sort of spiritual bacteria, that may, under certain conditions, find lodgement in men's souls, and germinate, as it were, in the *prima materia* of the brain, and be thus the fruitful seed of disease, and develop into actuality in the physical body. These morbid ideas, which are the true interior life of disease, are to be taken up, as we have before said, and borne away from the patient. So when the evil, the morbid idea, the *sin*, that lies at the root of the malady is removed, a vacuum is, as it were, formed, which God and nature are said to abhor, and the opposite good and truth, from a fixed divine law, flow in. A living, life-giving truth cannot be received until the error, the illusion, the *sin* which occupies the mind is removed. Healing, saving truth does not crowd out error or a false belief from the mind, nor neutralize it as an acid combines with an alkali to make a salt. But when the error or sin is removed, truth spontaneously flows in; when an evil is put away and ejected from the mind, we come into the opposite good. This is according to an established divine order. When we take up into our intellectual consciousness the morbid *idea* in the mind of the patient, or take upon ourselves intellectually, but not sensationally, his spiritual condition, we vicariously represent him in our own person, and bear that condition away from him, and prepare the soil of his soul for the reception of the *seed* of healing and saving truth. Thus did Jesus. He bore, or represented in his own person the sins of men. (I Pet. ii : 24.) He affirms that his works can be repeated by his followers. (John xiv : 12.) In the case of the cure of the paralytic, mentioned in the Gospel of Matthew, there are many valuable hints which can be taken advantage of in the psychological method of cure. One is that the remission of sin, or the banishment from the mind of a patient of the *error* or false *idea*, of which the disease is the physical counterpart or material expression, is equivalent to the cure of the malady. It is also affirmed that

God has given to the "son of man" — a purely Kabalistic expression for man, as to his soul-principle — power to do this. The spirit is the real man and son of God. The soul, as being generated by the spirit, is the son or offspring of the real man. This, when pervaded by the life of the spirit, has power on earth to bear away from the mind of another a false idea or sin. This is clearly taught in that remarkable passage in the Gospel of John, which contains a great truth and principle of Christianity which has been dropped out of the life of the church and forgotten. After the appearance of Jesus as a spirit to his disciples or scholars, he said to them, "As my father hath sent me, even so send I you. Whose soever sins ye remit (that is, banish, bear or send away), they are remitted unto them; and whose soever sins ye retain, they are retained." (John xx: 21, 22.) The term *sin* is here used in its radical sense, of an "aberration from the truth," or the divine reality of things, an error, a falsity, an illusion, and not in its corrupted theological signification. In this sense sin is the *psychic germ* of disease, the *idea* or living image of it, and that alone from which it can exist. The disciples of Jesus in all ages, through the coming to them of the Paraclete as the spirit and power of truth from him, and as the inward Word, which was to be inspired into them by his spiritual presence, were to be endowed with power to remit or *put away* sin, as being the cause of every physical malady, from the minds and life of men. How this is to be done in harmony with the laws of the mind has been shown above. We take up into ourself the morbid condition of the patient, and assume the psychic embryo of the disease, so that we vicariously represent him, and "bear it in our body up to the tree" (I Pet. ii: 24), — a profound Kabalistic expression. We take up into ourself his condition in order that we may form a clear idea of it, and this idea of it is the real disease, the *ding an sich*, or thing in itself. Thus we are able to remit it or put it away from him. This leaves in his mind a "peaceful vacancy," which the universal Divine Life and Light make haste to fill. This is the Messianic method of cure, and our skill and facility in doing this will prove to the world the curative efficiency of the psycho-therapeutic system of Jesus. There is a power in this psychological and transcendental method which few are prepared to admit.

It may aid us in understanding the deep philosophy of this method of cure, if we bear in mind that ideas are the only immediate objects of consciousness. In this Berkeley and Locke both agree. And it is a doctrine older than Plato, *that ideas are the only real things.* All real things belong to the "unseen world," or lie beyond the grasp of the senses. "Things seen," says Paul, "are temporal," are transient, evanescent, and unreal; "but things unseen (by the outward sense) are eternal." (II Cor. iv: 18.) Kant somewhere says that "the rose which we see is not the thing in itself, the *ding an sich,* but a phenomenon or appearance." The same is true of all the objects of nature and of man. You do not see the realities of things with the eye. I do not see my friend, but only what hides him from my sight. Man is always invisible to sense. I close my eyes and think of an absent friend, and I perceive a mental image of him, a living *idea* of him. This is the real man, the spiritual entity, the *ding an sich,* the thing in itself. This is the true doctrine of Platonic love, of which men speak without knowing what it means. Says Plotinus, "As long as some one is conversant with that figure only which is manifest to the eyes, he does not yet love the object which he sees; but when departing from it, he generates in himself, in his impartible (indivisible) soul, a form which is not an object of sense, then love springs forth." (*Plotinus,* translated by Thomas Taylor, p. 92.) That is the love of the real person or thing. It is only by closing the eyes, or by freeing the soul from the trammels of the physical senses, that we see, in the interior light, things in themselves. Perhaps blind persons see more realities than we see, for the reason that what we call vision is but a veil drawn over our real sight. Jesus, the Christ, refers to this, when he says of the sensuous Jewish rabble, "that having eyes, they saw not, and having ears they heard not." The understanding — the intellectual soul-principle — is the true organ of vision. It is that which lies back of the eye, and is represented by the eye. "The light of the body," says Jesus, "is the eye (intellect), if thine eye is simple, or not compound, that is, if we see with the intellect alone without the external organ, our whole body, or soul, is full of light." The whole soul becomes an organ of vision, and all the five senses are reduced to a unity, an indefinable perception of ideas, the spiritual and real side of things.

What men call disease has a spiritual side to it, an *ideal reality*. The external is the apparent and phenomenal, the shadow and not the substance. If the spiritual idea of it is the real side of it, and if we can take this up into ourselves, and bear it away from the mind of the patient, it is easy to see that he would be redeemed from it.

But it must be kept in mind that this method of cure which was practised by Jesus implies in the patient a *desire* to be saved, and a *predisposition to believe*. Where these exist, the cure is easy. Where they do not exist, little can be done, and it is a waste of time and energy to undertake impossibilities. We often witness the efficiency of this ideal method of cure where it is instinctively employed without an intelligent comprehension of its principles. How often does the mother, when her child has fallen down and inflicted upon himself a slight bruise, lift him gently up, pass her hand over the place, take up the idea of it into herself, and by dispersive movements of the hand put it away, as it were, saying to the child, "Now it is all gone," and telling him to jump up and run. That is quite frequently the last ever heard from it, for the cure is complete. But in this whole transaction there lies concealed a deeper philosophy than the world in general has ever recognized.

Every person is surrounded by an emanative sphere of his life. This is represented by the aureola or nimbus around the heads of saints and divinities in pictures and medals. Especially is this seen in the pictures of Jesus. This is a circle or disk of rays invisible to our crude senses, but plainly perceptible to our inner vision, and is by no means a mere creation of fancy having no substantial reality, but represents what actually exists in every person — an emanative sphere of our thoughts and feelings; in other words, of our life. It is different in different persons, and in the same person at different times, as it is always in correspondence with our inward states. In all depressing mental conditions, as, for instance, in melancholy, this *nimbus* or sombre exhalation is to be removed by dispersive passes, which is one of the most effectual ways of changing the morbid mental condition of a patient, and of expunging from his mind the *idea* and *misbelief* which constitute the invisible side of his malady. This is the teaching of the ancient arcane science of magnetism, and the experience of many thousands of years has placed it among established principles and demonstrated its efficiency. It is now given to the world for the benefit of humanity. By removing the dark cloud (so to speak) or the odyllic emanation that surrounds the brain, — and it is as easily done as you can quench the flame of a candle with a sweep of the hand, — you prepare the way for the reception of a higher and better influx. Just as when you brush away the air around your face with a fan, fresh air immediately flows in to take its place.

This principle is given with an actual experimental knowledge of its practical value, though to our modern materialistic science of medicine it may seem of no importance. It has been said by some one "that Jesus cured disease by purifying the atmosphere both *within* and without the patient."

This he could do by the power of the inner Word and the Spirit, and by these divine agencies we may learn in our feebler way to do the same. A knowledge of the science of magnetism is of great advantage to the practitioner of the mental cure system. To cure disease by the phrenopathic method, while wholly ignoring magnetism, must seem to many persons like professing to fly without wings, or like an attempt to practise telegraphy and denouncing the battery and the wire, but all the time using both while kept out of sight. But it must be borne in mind, that the most efficient and successful use of the principle of magnetism does not imply *contact* with a patient. The establishment of this principle is one of the things done for the science by the celebrated and world-renowned Baron Du Potet, the prince of modern magnetists, and who is worthy to be named with Pythagoras, with Apollonius of Tyana, and with Paracelsus, and Van Helmont. Magnetism in the old spiritual science is identical with the *universal life-principle*, and is the medium through which our minds influence the minds of others, and a thought and will impulse are transmissible. To undertake to affect the mind of another without it is as absurd as to attempt to communicate sound through an absolute vacuum, or for a skilful mechanic to go forth to his work, but leave his tools behind.

CHAPTER XXI.

THE SUMMIT OF CHRISTIAN KNOWLEDGE, OR THE MYSTERY OF THE CHRIST, AND ITS SAVING INFLUENCE.

PAUL declares that he counted all things as loss, and even as useless refuse, in comparison with the excellency of the knowledge of Christ. He joyfully suffered the loss of all things that he might win (or gain) Christ, and *be found in Him*, not having his own righteousness, which is of the law, and which is only apparent and not real; but that righteousness which is from, or out of, God, through faith in Christ. (Phil. iii: 8, 9.) This places the knowledge of Christ at the summit of human thought, and makes it the *summum bonum*, or supreme good of the human heart. This is not an exaggeration, but a sober divine truth, — an infinite fact and reality. To be consciously in Christ is to be a new creature or creation, that is, it is the birth of a new and higher man in us. It is to merge our individual and partial self in the higher Self, our Ego in the absolute Ego. Paul attained to this conception. In the Epistle to the Galatians he says: "I am crucified with Christ (a Kabalistic expression), nevertheless I live, yet not I, but the Christ liveth in me." (Col. ii: 20.) He found himself included in the Christ, as the divine Collective Man, and by virtue of this conjunction, was *complete* in Him who is the head of all principality and power; for in him is the first personal manifestation of the "Unknown," and all the fulness of God. (Col. ii: 10.) All human spirits are included in the being of the Christ, who is the Universal Spirit, and have gone forth from Him without going out of Him so as to lose their connection with Him. The intuitive recognition of this sublime truth in all its far-reaching significance, and in all its practical saving influence, is the highest act of faith. We have shown in a preceding lesson the importance of separating by an act of judgment, our real self, the immortal Ego, from the disease that afflicts us. But it is the completion of this act of faith, and its crowning position, to find our real self included in the Absolute Self, or personage which Paul denominates the Christ, who is the first and only man, as all other men as to their spirits are but repetitions or modified manifestations of Him.

This leads us to inquire, "Who and what is the Christ of Paul?" This is called a *mystery*, by which is not meant an incomprehensible doctrine, or unknowable truth, but one not generally revealed; in fact, only made known to the "perfect," or those fully instructed. Paul received this knowledge by direct revelation from the risen and ascended Jesus more fully than any and all the other apostles. It was a special dispensation of the "grace" of God to him, as one fitted by his previous studies to receive it and fully apprehend it. He tells us how by revelation was made known to him the mystery, which, when we read, we may perceive his understanding in the mystery of the Christ which in other generations had not been made known unto the sons of men, as it was then revealed unto his holy apostles and prophets in the Spirit. (Eph. iii: 2–4.) It was a doctrine concealed from the masses and veiled from their understanding by a symbolic covering, for the idea of communicating spiritual knowledge to the unthinking multitude did not belong to the ancient civilization. He declares also that the great mystery of the Gospel, and a truth which had been generally hidden from mankind during all preceding ages and generations was then made known unto the saints, which is Christ *in* us, the hope of glory. (Col. i: 26, 27.) The rescuing these truths from the inner sanctuary and the priestly caste, and making them the common property of mankind, was the real offence of Jesus, and the one for which he suffered death. Thus he died for the benefit of all men everywhere. But the question still recurs, "Who is Christ, and what is it to be *in* Him, and to have Him *in* us?" We will now reverently approach and lift at least a corner of the veil from this great mystery, the deepest, the most satisfying, and the most influentially saving of all knowledge that lies within the reach of human thought. If we get but a glimpse of it, it will be in our consciousness the dawn of a new day, the beginning of a new *creation*.

In all the archaic wisdom-religions, the Hindu, the Egyptian, the Chaldean, and also the Judaic and early Christian, there lies back of all creation or manifested existence, the "Unknown God," the supreme Divine Essence, the Swayambhuva of the Hindus, or the Aditi, the Absolute, the Unbounded, as it is defined by Max Müller; the same who is called in the Chaldean and Jewish Kabala, the En Soph, the No Thing. It is perhaps the Father of Jesus, whom no man knoweth, only so far as he is revealed in the Son. Out of this "Invisible God," as he is called by Paul, all creation springs, but by an order and law that is called emanative causality. Each successive emanation from the Unknown Abyss, or each out-going universal principle, is less and less subjective, and more and more external and comparatively unreal, and matter is the remotest effect and ultimate boundary of the emanative energy, beyond which is the *No Thing* again. The Christ of Paul is the first, and includes all the others in himself. He is the Alpha and Omega, the first and the last, and all between the extremes. In that truly Kabalistic book, the Apocalypse of John, the Christ is called "the beginning of the creation of God." (Rev. iii : 15.) It will be borne in mind that Paul was familiar with the secret doctrines of the Jews, as they are given in the Kabala of Simon Ben Jochai, and a slight knowledge of this explains many of those things, which, as Peter affirms, are hard to be understood in his Epistles. In the scheme of the Ten Sephiroth, or Emanations, or Hypostases, the first is the Crown, the Crest or Apex of all created existence, and which is *pure thought* and the principle of thought. This is the Primordial Point, the initial act and principle of creation. This divides itself into two rays: a Father and a Mother ray, a masculine and feminine principle and potency, the *Nous* and the *Sophia*. The union of these is the Son of God, the first man, the God-Man and the Man-God, the Adam Kadmon of the Kabala, called also Protogonos, or First Begotten. It is the Archetypal Man of Plato, or of man as he exists in the divine Idea. All things and all worlds are contained in him, and go forth from him without going out of him. Hence the tendency of all things, in their return toward their source, to assume the *human form*. As the Kabala expresses it, the mineral becomes a plant, the plant an animal the animal a man, and man becomes divine. This is the Divine Man, the Christ of Paul, at the same time a divine personage and a universal *humanized principle* of life and light. In the Epistle to the Colossians, which contains a fuller expression of the Christology of Paul than any other of his Epistles, he says of the Christ, " Who is the *image* of the *Invisible God*, the *firstborn of all creation*, for *in him* were all things created, in the heavens and upon the earth, things visible and invisible, whether thrones, or dominions, or principalities, or powers, all things have been created through him and unto (or *in*) him; and he is before all things, and by him all things consist" (or *hold together*). (Col. i : 15–18.) This is the Kabala with the veil removed. In the first emanation from the " Unknown," the Maximus Homo, or greatest man of Swedenborg, and the Christ of Paul, all men and all things are included, like a body made up of innumerable parts, each of which is an *image* of the whole. We are in him, only more really so, in the same way that the artist creates the picture or the statue first in himself. This is an ideal but real entity, without which the material expression of it could not exist. This idea is the immortal part of it. The material manifestation of it may be marred or destroyed, but this, never. This ideal and real man which I am in Christ, the archetypal man, has the force of *destiny*, not meaning fate, but an intelligent and benevolent plan of my life, which has its use in the grand economy of being. It is only when we perceive by faith that we are included in the being of the Divine Man, Christ, that we are complete, or filled out to the full expression of the divine idea of man. Our weak and imperfect self is merged in the grand unity of the divine-human principle, the divine humanity of the Lord, which is the Christ. Our life is no longer an isolated fragment of life, but is merged in the whole. When that which is perfect (or universal) is come, then that which is in part is done away. The individual, isolated Ego disappears, and our life is hid with Christ in God. (Col. iii: 3.) Or, as it is expressed by Jesus in relation to those who believe on him, "I in them and thou in me, that they may be perfected into one." (John xvii: 23.) As our true being is in the Christ, he gives his life to us, and permits us to call his life and his righteousness our own, and to appropriate it as such. Just as if each member of our body were an express image of the body, and the life of the whole circulated through it. This finding of our real self in the Christ is the perfect state of man, or of man returned to the state whence he started into existence. There is a Divine Human Principle and Personage that is the inmost life of all that is in the heavens and the earths. There is an unbroken chain of being, from the moss to the angel, and each individual link, though it has a form of life peculiar to itself, is yet a manifestation of the life of the whole. As it has been eloquently said, "the last, highest, brightest link of this chain, and which conjoins it to the Deity, is man; the incarnation of thought itself, which is the summation of the universe; man, that includes in himself all other links and their single secret, the personified universe, the subject of the world." (J. H. STIRLING in his triumphant reply to Huxley, *Half Hours with Modern Scientists*, series ii., p. 137.)

The universal spirit is the proximate or first emanation from the "Unknown," and is the Universal Man, or a divine human principle, and my spirit, which is my immortal self, is an individualized manifestation of the whole, a finite limitation of it, without being sundered from it. Philo, the Jewish mystic and philosopher, and a contemporary of Jesus, calls the Logos, who is the manifested Christ, *the true man*, ὁ ἀληθινὸς ἄνθρωπος. Viewing myself as a disconnected fragment of the whole, and on the plane of sense becoming blind to the invisible tie which binds me to the whole, I may be weak, and diseased, and sinful. But when by faith I connect my real self with the supreme and perfect Man, as if a drop were returned to the ocean, without ceasing to be a drop, then I am whole or complete. I am now included in Christ; I have found my real self in Christ, and have become a new and higher creation, as all who thus believe in Christ are taken up into Christ and incorporated into him, and he is never sick or sinful. This is the Christ of Paul, and his conception of a life of faith in him. It is not strange that he denominated it a mystery, and that he should suffer the loss of all things that he might win (or gain) Christ and be found *in* him. This is the priceless pearl or spiritual truth of the kingdom of the heavens, in order to purchase which a man sells all other things, and finds it cheap at that. For when my immortal Ego, my inner and real self, is intuitively perceived to be in Christ, it represents the grand unity of spirit, or man as the image and Son of God, just as a drop of the ocean possesses all the qualities and properties of the great deep, and is, as it were, the ocean concentrated into a drop. This is according to that sublime axiom of the Hermetic philosophy, *Omnia ex Uno, Omnia in Uno, Omnia ad Unum, Omnia per Medium, et Omnia in Omnibus*, All things out of One, All things in One, All things tend to One, All things through an Intermediate, and All things in All. It was the doctrine of Paul, that to be in Christ, or to intuitively view our individual spirit and real self as included in the Christ, just as the atmosphere of this room, while it receives form and limitation from the room, is nevertheless inseparable from the boundless air, raises man to a plane of thought and conscious life that is inconsistent with sin and disease. This idea and disease cannot coëxist in our consciousness on this exalted elevation. By this faith man is lifted up to a spiritual altitude, far above that sensuous stratum of our being where sin, disease, and death are possible. This is Paul's resurrection in Christ and with Christ. If this is an eternal truth, and not the baseless fabric of a dream, then why need we look any further for a remedy for either soul or body? By this Pauline doctrine, we are brought under the branches of the tree of life, and may pluck and eat and live forever, for the Kabalistic "tree of life" is none other than the first man, the Christ of Paul.

The Christ is not only a manifestation of the Divine Intellect, or highest intelligence, but also of the Divine Love, a love that passes knowledge, an infinite and irrepressible inclination to impart his own good and truth to all. And the Christian method of salvation is to find in the Christ all that we need, and to appropriate it or make it our own by *faith*. Christ, as we have said, is the Archetypal Man, or man as he exists in the Divine Idea. And this idea contains in its essence a *conatus* to realize itself in every human being. The Christ within is in an endeavor to pass outward into an ultimate expression, and save even the body.

The next degree of emanation below the Christ of Paul, and which brings the "Unknown" one discrete degree nearer to us, is the Logos or Word, as it was called by Philo and the Alexandrian Platonists. It is also so named in the prologue of the Gospel of John, and is represented as the active principle of creation, and the true light that lighteth every man that cometh into the world. In it is life, and the life is the light of men. (John i: 1-14.) He is the Pímander of Hermes, the Viradj of the Hindus. In the Kabala he is called the Angel Metatron, the mediatorial principle. He is the Angel of Jehovah of the Old Testament, and by an angel is meant an emanative principle or that which is sent forth from God. He is the Presence Angel in whom was the *name* of God. The Word is the source of all knowledge and all goodness in the *rational soul* of man. All truth in us is Christ as the Word. Thus, as Paul expresses it, he is made unto us wisdom from (or out of) God, and righteousness (or faith), and sanctification, and redemption. (I Cor. i: 30.) This manifestation of God as the "Word" is the inward voice, "*the still small voice,*" that Elijah heard within. It is what men call conscience, but it does not merely teach what is right and what is wrong, but gives us an intuitive perception of all truth that lies above and beyond the range of the sensuous mind. The Logos is identical with the *Daimonion*, or inward teacher of Sokrates. It is the inner light of the Quietists and the Society of Friends. The abode of the Logos is the "intelligible world" of Plato, and the *rational soul* in man belongs to this plane or sphere of being. This world, which is personified in the Logos, is the repository of all spiritual knowledge. All that was ever known or can be known is there in idea, and may by influx flow into the rational soul of man, as the flower absorbs and appropriates the dew or the everywhere present moisture of the atmosphere. The sages and initiates of the inner sanctuary claimed to possess the secret of absorbing knowledge without intellectual effort by simply holding the soul open passively to receive it, and it could be assimilated so as to become a part of themselves.

The next manifestation of God, and the lowest or most external divine *triad*, is the Adonai or the Lord, the Universal Life-Principle, the *Anima Mundi*, and nearly the same as the Holy Spirit. The Lord is the divinely intelligent principle that creates and governs the material universe, and is its only life and force, but who has infinite depths of being beyond all sensible phenomena. In the Kabalistic Ten Sephiroth, the lowest *triad* is made up of Hod (splendor), and Netzah (firmness), answering in us to understanding and will. These masculine and feminine principles are united in Jesod (foundation), the Mighty Living One, being the corresponding name of God. The three personified are the Adonai, the Lord of life. Swedenborg, from the Hermetic philosophy, everywhere affirms and continually reiterates the truth that there is but one Life in the heavens and upon the earth, and that Life is the *Lord*. From this everywhere present Life springs the *instinctive intelligence* of plants, animals, and men. The Christ is the principle of illumination in the *Spirit* of man, the Logos of the *rational soul*, and the Lord, as the *welt-geist*, or world spirit, of the psychical nature. The Christ, as the Adonai or Lord, is the inward teacher of the mind on the plane of sense, quickening, exalting, and rightly interpreting all our sense perceptions, and removing the veil from truths symbolically expressed. Under this view he is presented to us by Paul in the Second Epistle to the Corinthians, where he says, that when the Old Testament is read, there is a veil upon the heart of the Jews which prevents their perceiving its esoteric or interior meaning, like the sun obscured by a cloud. "But whenever a man shall turn to the Lord, the veil is taken away. Now the Lord is the Spirit: and where the Spirit of the Lord is, there is liberty (or freedom from the bondage of sense). But we all with unveiled face, beholding as in a mirror, the glory of the Lord, are transformed into the same image from glory to glory, even as from the Lord the Spirit." (II Cor. iii: 14-18. New version.)

This doctrine of the Christ, and our relation to Him, is a Platonic doctrine. Says Dr. Ackermann, "The safest way to a living apprehension of the Platonic *Idea* proceeds from the *true apprehension of impersonality in consciousness*, and this in its relation to the Godhead. He who grasps himself *in thought*, and apprehends and finds *himself in himself* and at the same time *in another*, viz., in God, to him it will no longer be obscure and unintelligible what Plato meant by ideas." (*Christian Element in Plato*, p. 186.) It is a doctrine much older than Plato, and existed in the minds of men as a saving truth before the foundation of the pyramids was laid.

CHAPTER XXII.

THE RELATION OF JESUS TO THE CHRIST AND TO MAN.

AFTER what has been said in the preceding section, it only remains to say a few words respecting the relation of Jesus to the Christ of Paul. As all human minds are connected through a universal mind, through Jesus as an inlet the Christ entered into humanity, and deposited in it the germ of a new and higher life. In a preëminent degree, he was an incarnation of the Christ,—not that no one else ever was, for all spiritually enlightened mind is a manifestation of the Christ and the Word. But owing to the unexampled spiritual evolution of the man Jesus, his individual life became merged and blended into a unity with the "Only-Begotten of the Father," the Universal Christ. In him also the Word was made flesh or manifested on the psychical plane of mind, and we beheld his glory. And his intelligent mastery of the natural forces indicated his union with the Adonai or Lord who has all power in the heavens and the earth. In Jesus we witness a complete humanized expression of the Christ, the Word and the Spirit. His personality is an inlet and an outlet of those universal divine principles, and a medium through which they may enter into each one of us, and through which the human race may have access to them. In him and through him we may have an actual communication with the Christ, " in whom are hid all the treasures of wisdom and knowledge," as we can have through no other man of human history. If this is true (and I fully believe it is), why need we go any farther to find all the instruction we need in the divine science of spiritual things. Coming into sympathetic relation with him, I am brought into conjunction with the fountain of all true wisdom, and it may flow into my mind according to the degree of my receptivity. For neither Jesus or the Christ have ever removed out of hailing nearness to the human spirit. In his second coming or advent as the Paraclete, "the Spirit of truth," he promised to teach his disciples all things and guide them into all truth; in fact, to make known to us those many things concerning the mysteries of the kingdom of God, which he had to say, but men were not then able to receive. There is no doubt that all that was ever known by man still exists in the world of mind, and through Jesus may be communicated to the spirit of man; so that there is nothing hid, no occult wisdom, that may not be revealed. For Jesus was and is familiar with it all, and it is the nature and animus of Christianity to make what was confined to the few in past ages the common property of man. It is but three steps upward to communion with the Highest. Jesus conducts us to the Christ, and the Christ to the Father. He has been lifted up or elevated on the mystic cross, — not merely the wood of Calvary, the place of skulls, but the Hermetic cross as "the tree of life,"— and from his spiritual altitude he is drawing all men unto him. (John xii: 32.) Jesus represents not merely an Oriental Christ, but the Universal Messiah or anointing One. What he said to one he said to all mind in that condition. (Mark xiii: 37.) No word he ever uttered can be lost beyond recall. (John xiv: 26.) It still exists in mind. In Jesus as a man raised up to represent all humanity, the Christ touched with a vivifying contact our psychical nature, and that need not be suppressed by extreme ascetic mortifications, as is done in Brahmanism, and the lower Buddhism, but may be lifted up entire, as Moses symbolically lifted up the *serpent* in the wilderness, the representative of the sensual principle in man. So in Jesus, every "son of man" — a Kabalistic expression for the human soul — may be elevated from a mere sensuous or psychical plane of thought to a true spiritual life, with all its tranquil blessedness. An invocation directed to Jesus will reach the listening ear of an ever-present and never-distant Christ. The Christ of whom I have spoken might seem to many to be too abstract a conception, too transcendental, until men are raised to a higher spiritual level. But in Jesus we have a principle of mediation. In him the Christ becomes objective, and through him my thought-utterances and heart-cravings may reach the heart of the Christ, as certainly as the sound vibrations of my voice may be heard by my friend, far removed from my sight, through the telephonic wire and its ethereal vibrations. After long and patient study of the Christ of Paul and his relation to the human spirit, the real life of man, and the relation of Jesus to the Christ and to humanity, I can say to the world, as the inspired apostles said to the Jews on the day of Pentecost, "Let all the house of Israel know assuredly that God hath made this Jesus whom ye crucified both Lord and Christ." (Acts ii: 36.) And if any one asks, What must I do to be saved (or healed of sin and disease), the shortest, most definite, and divinely efficacious prescription I could give is, "Believe in the *name* of the Lord Jesus Christ, and thou shalt be saved." Believe in him for all his name implies. For Jesus is presented to us in the Christian system as able to save to the uttermost (or to the remotest boundary of our being, the body) all that come unto God by him, seeing he ever liveth to make intercession for us (or to execute the divinely established function of mediation between us and the only saving power in the universe, and which is concealed in his *name*). If he cannot save, I know not where to look, or to whom to apply. In the *formula fidei* or condensed expression of faith of Buddhism, which is called *Trisharana* or "the three refuges," it is said, "I take my refuge in Buddha, Dharma, and Samgha." By Dharma is meant the doctrines, teachings, and precepts of Gautama. Samgha signifies the assemblies and ritualistic observances of the Church. After a careful study, pursued without prejudice, of the system of Buddhism, both in its theoretical and practical aspects, while acknowledging in it much that is divinely true, and identical with Christianity, I am still constrained to say, "I take my refuge in Jesus the Christ." In every age of the world God has raised up extraordinary men, and imparted to them a high degree of light from the living Word. Such was Moses, Zoroaster, Confucius, Plato, and above all Gautama the Buddha. There was many a stray beam of the living light of the Logos in all their systems, but it does not come in a form to be easily and practically appropriated by the souls of men in general. And if Jesus should say to me as he did to the twelve select disciples, when many of his shallow followers were leaving him, "Will you also go away?" I should be constrained to say, as all the world's great teachers passed in procession before the mind, "Lord, to whom shall I go? Thou hast the words of eternal life." (John vi: 68.) In Jesus we may come into saving contact with the "Word of Life." (I John i: 2.) In no person was there ever so conscious a union with God, as even Renan affirms. The philosopher Porphyry was united to God, as he says, but twice in his life, while his teacher Plotinus had been six times. They had come to the perception of their own inner divine spirit, the *Augoeides*, or shining One, of the philosopher initiates. But a conscious and inseparable union with God was the normal condition of Jesus. And there is no shorter or better route to the attainment of the highest spiritual light and life than a sympathetic conjunction with Jesus, the Way, the Truth, and the Life. For that eternal Life which was with the Father is manifested in him, and brought within our grasp. In the Pauline development of Christianity, when rescued from the dogmas of a theology that has been grafted upon it, and freed from the shell of exoteric Judaism and restored to its primitive meaning, we find God's response to our soul's inmost needs. It is the power of God and the wisdom of God unto salvation for both soul and body, to every one that believeth.

But, according to Paul, my salvation in Christ is not to be viewed as an event to transpire in a distant or near future, but a genuine faith apprehends and appropriates it as an eternally existing fact. "The *head* of every man is Christ, and the head of Christ is God." (I Cor. xi: 3.) That is, the highest region of our being, the immortal Ego, and real *self*, is inseparable from the Christ, the God-Man, and the Man-God, and that spiritual and divine entity was never lost, or diseased, or unhappy. It is not the head, the summit of human nature, the spirit, that needs to be washed or cleansed. That is already pure; but it is the feet, the animal soul; and if these are washed, we are then clean every whit. This is one of those profound sayings of Jesus that even the apostles did not understand until they were initiated more fully into the mysteries of the kingdom of God. (John xiii: 4–10.) All men were created in Christ, as I have before said, something as an artist creates his picture or statue, in *idea*. This is the real and immortal entity. So in Christ; or, as "a man in Christ," as Paul expresses it, I am perfect and complete. This is the true idea of my existence, the divine plan of my life. If I believe this of myself and of Christ, and steadfastly maintain this idea and belief, it will work itself out into an ultimate expression, and translate itself into even a bodily manifestation. This *idea* of ourselves has been lost to our consciousness, and the divine plan may have been temporarily marred. But Paul teaches that we may be created anew in Christ Jesus unto good works, which God before ordained that we should walk in them. (Eph. 2: 10.) Through Jesus, the divine *ideal* becomes the actual. Every one of us was made for a use in the grand economy of the universe. To find out what we are created for, and to do that use, is our highest health and happiness. Jesus sought to find in those he healed the true idea of their being, and to so create them anew as to make it an actuality. We should do the same.

It has been said of Gautama the Buddha, that his life is "the history of a soul in search of spiritual rest, of the various experiments by which he vainly sought to find it, of the success that at last crowned his efforts, and finally of his life-long endeavor to communicate to others the blessing he seemed to himself to have obtained." The answer of Buddhism to the inquiry,

> "O where shall rest be found,
> Rest for the weary soul?"

is in the extinction or "snuffing out" of desire. Desire, it is said, begets will, and will is force, and force is matter, and matter is evil. So the descent from desire to matter and unrest is in as direct a line downward as that pursued by an apple in falling from the tree to the ground. There is much of truth in this. The answer of Jesus, speaking as the Christ, is "Come unto (or up to) me, all ye that labour and are heavy laden, and I will give you rest." (Mat. xi : 28-30.) In the doctrine of the Christ and of his relation to me as constituting my inner and true self, we find a secure refuge from sin and disease. When, by a supreme act of faith, I perceive that my spiritual self is included in him, as the Collective or Universal Man, I have found *myself*, and found it *in* Christ, as Paul expresses it. So far as I *believe* this it becomes to me a conscious reality, and in him I am possessed of all good that can be an object of desire, and have nothing to ask. (John xvi : 23.) We have reached the true Nirvana, or snuffing out of desire, when we can say, —

> "Thou, O Christ, art all I want,
> More than all in thee I find."

This is not so much an extinction of desire, as it is its complete satisfaction and fulfilment. As disease in its essence, as the word radically signifies, is a state of unrest and disquietude, when I have found my real self in Christ, and in him every need is met, I am in a state of true health.

> "Now rest, my long divided heart,
> Fixed on this blissful centre, rest,
> Nor ever from thy Lord depart,
> With him of every good possessed."

No one was ever entirely satisfied with himself until he finds his real self; and, as Plotinus would express it, the man that I am here is united to the man that exists in True Being, or the Christ. But why was man from a pure spirit reduced to the bondage of the senses, and imprisoned in matter? The reason is given by Paul in the Epistle to the Romans. The intelligent creation, or man as an intelligent spiritual being, was made subject to *vanity* (which is the *maia* or illusion of the senses and of matter of the Buddhists), not willingly on our part, and consequently it is not what we are condemned for, but it was done by the reason of Him who hath subjected us to this in hope of deliverance. For the "creature," says Paul, shall be delivered from the bondage of corruption into the glorious liberty of the sons of God, which is the designation of man as a pure spiritual intelligence. Then he will connect in his own personality the two extreme links of existence, the Alpha and the Omega, or spirit and matter. The evils and sufferings of our present sensuous condition are only travailing pains that are followed by the birth of a higher state. (Rom. viii : 18-22.) All this was taught Kabalistically or symbolically in one of the early chapters of the Book of Genesis. The marriage of the Benai Eloheim or sons of God, which represents our spiritual nature, with the "daughters of men," the *psyche* of the Greeks, or the mind on the sensuous and material plane, gives birth to a higher race, mighty men, and men of renown. From this union of our higher with the so-called lower nature, we have a race of men who can consciously dwell in the world of sense and at the same time in the realm of spirit, like Jesus " the son of man who *is* in heaven."

CHAPTER XXIII.

THE KABALISTIC JUSTICE AND PAUL'S RIGHTEOUSNESS OF FAITH, AND THEIR CURATIVE POWER.

In the philosophy of Plato and the Oriental Theosophy the word "justice" had an occult meaning far transcending its ordinary signification. In the popular mind it had, and still has, the same meaning as *equity*, but among the philosopher initiates it was something more, and much more. Plato says in the "Cratylus" that he learned from the *sacred mysteries* that justice is the same as cause, it being the most *penetrating* of all things. But in stating this, he says, he seems " to inquire farther than is becoming, and to pass beyond the trench." He therefore puts it into the mouths of others, of whom he asks the meaning of the word, to give its full signification. One man gives it as his opinion that justice is the sun, because the sun's light penetrates and influences everything, meaning of course the spiritual sun, whose light is pure truth. Another is made to say that justice is that intellect of which Anaxagoras speaks when he affirms that intellect — by which he means a pure deific or spiritual intelligence — orders and is the cause of all things. It is a rectitude of thought, a perception of things on the square, to use a Masonic symbol. These higher intellectual perceptions, uninfluenced by the illusions of the senses, and which are the rays of a divine intelligence, are "the righteousness of faith" of which Paul speaks. It is the faith *of* the Christ, the intellectual perception that belongs to the crest or summit of our being. It is the faith of the "Son of God," the Kabalistic designation of our inmost spirit. It is at the same time a deific intelligence and a deific power, because it is a manifestation in us of the same intellect that creates and governs the world. According to Plato, our *gnostic* or knowing powers exist in three degrees. The lowest is mere animal instinct, and reason, and *opinion*, which may be true or false. The next higher degree is *faith*, which is far more than opinion and that degree of knowledge which is called *science*, which is a superficial perception of external facts. The highest of all is *intuition*, which is the divine light that illuminates the inmost or supreme man or mind. This is an intelligence invested with a large fraction of God's omnipotence.

It is also said by Plato in the "Timæus"— and it is a fundamental doctrine of the ancient Theosophy — that there are two classes of things of which our minds are cognizant; first, things that exist in *true being*, or those that have a *real* existence, and are, as Kant would call them, "things in themselves." These are *ideas*. Secondly, there are things that are in a state of "becoming to be," but really are not. These include all our sense-perceptions and the objects of the so-called external world. They are not realities, but only their appearances or resemblances. These are recognized by *opinion*, — which is only a little elevated above the animal life, — conjoined with irrational sense. The other class of things, or those that have *true being*, are apprehended by pure intellect, which, as we have seen, is identical with the Kabalistic "justice" and Paul's righteousness of faith. The word so often used by Paul, δικιοσύνη, and which is in our common version translated "justification," is the understanding of the *just man*, as Plato asserts, or the attainment of pure intelligence. Dr. Ackermann, in his "Christian Element in Plato," says that the Platonic meaning of ἁμαρτία (*hamartia*), sin, is an error of the understanding, and we must suppose that Plato and even Paul understood Greek. By sin is meant the illusion and erroneous judgment of the senses, which is always the direct opposite of the truth, or that clear intelligence which is called justice and faith. Paul says, "Let not *sin* reign in your mortal bodies," that is, let not these erroneous and illusory judgments of the mind on the plane of irrational sense control the corporeal condition. But let grace (or *occult wisdom*, as the word Kabalistically means) reign unto righteousness, through Jesus Christ our Lord. (Rom. v : 21.)

In every case of disease it is incumbent on us to ask, whether it belongs to things that *really are*, or those which have an existence in our true being, or to the class of things which includes all our sense perceptions, that only *appear* to be, but really are not. It is our right to appeal the case from the court of irrational sense, with all its phantasms, to a higher intellectual tribunal, — to the decision of the Platonic and Kabalistic justice, and Paul's "righteousness of faith," where the decision of the mind on the plane of sense will be reversed, and the disease will be classed among illusions, deceptive appearances, or sin which has no right to reign in our mortal body. This is only following the precept of Jesus, " judge not according to appearance (sight, sense), but judge righteous judgment"; or, according to the true nature of things, which is always the direct opposite of the decision of the sensuous mind. Faith in the above sense, as the perception of truth which is above and beyond the grasp of the senses, would seem to be the divinely appointed remedy for the maladies of the soul, from which the diseases of the body arise, and of which they are the corporeal expression. In the "Timæus," Plato says, "that the disease of the soul is folly, or a privation of pure intellect. But there are two kinds of folly, the one madness, the other ignorance. Whatever influence therefore introduces either of these must be called disease." (*Works of Plato*, by Thomas Taylor, p. 544.) If this is true, it irresistibly follows that the most efficient remedy for the soul's ailments must be real truth, and the perception of truth that lies above and beyond the plane of sense, and that puts our minds on the same exalted level with that divine intellect that creates and governs the world, is the Kabalistic justice, and Paul's righteousness of faith or rectitude of thought. This pure thought uninfluenced by sense, which separates the disease from our true being, and views our real self as exempt from all evil, is a silent but omnipotent energy that is the sovereign panacea for the maladies of the soul and its body. He who has the most of it comes nearest to the Christ, before whose name every knee bows, or owns allegiance.

The doctrine of the triune nature of man has always been the teaching of the spiritually minded of all ages and countries of the world. It is a doctrine of which we must never lose sight, and it must be to us something more than an *opinion;* it must become to us an intuitive perception, as it was to the mystics of the middle ages, — as Ruysbroek, Eckart, and Tauler. They looked upon human nature as tripartite, like the three stories of a house, or like the temple of Solomon, which is more a symbolic than a historic edifice. There is in man, first, the outer court of sense; next, the inner sanctuary of the intellectual soul; and lastly, in the East, the most holy place, the spirit, where, like the high priest, we may commune with God. This is the inmost region of our being, and our *real* self. It is included *in* the Christ, or the Universal Spirit. On this subject, Ruysbroek says, "I believe that the Son is the image of the Father, that in the Son have dwelt from all eternity, foreknown and contemplated by the Father, the prototypes (or ideas) of all mankind. We existed in the Son before we were born. He is the creative ground of all creatures, — the eternal cause and principle of their life. The highest essence of our being rests therefore in God, — exists in his image in the Son." (Vaughn's *Hours with the Mystics*, Vol. I., p. 25.) This summit of our being, which is the real and divine man, is never contaminated by evil, nor invaded by disease. The recognition of this truth, and the separation in thought of sin and disease from our inmost and only true self, is the Platonic (and also the Pauline) idea of redemption. Says Dr. Ackermann, "It is evident what Plato means by redemption, or how he conceives this event in the life of the soul. He thinks of it as *a coming to one's self*, an apprehending of one's self as (truly) existent, as a severing of the inmost being from the surrounding element, as a separation of one's self from the changing mass of the world and life, *as a concretization of the original spiritual element in man to a divinely illuminated germ of light and life.*" (*Christian Element in Plato*, p. 247.) This coming to ourself, or the discovery of our true being, as in the case of the prodigal son, is the first step in our return to the Father, and the finding of this self not only in one's self, but also at the same time in another and higher being; that is, *in God in Christ*, is the Christian and Pauline idea of Salvation in the full sense of the word. We are expected and taught by the pulpit and the Church to find our real self, and to view it as polluted by sin, from the crown of the head to the soles of our feet. But this is the direct opposite of the truth. It was one of the doctrines of the Hermetic philosophers of all ages, among whom we unhesitatingly class Paul, that there centrally dwells in human nature the *voice* of the Divine Wisdom. This is the Genius Optimus, the Daimonion or divine guide of Sokrates, our inmost divine spirit and true self, the "Soul of the Soul," and the all-seeing eye of the mind. It is that part or region of man that is incapable of contamination or damnation, and is never affected by evil and never lost, even in the greatest of sinners. This is even said to have been Cromwell's firm reliance and belief, and his last question to his attending chaplain bore reference to the assurance of it. In most men it is latent, and is as unknown to consciousness as the interior of the pyramid of Cheops, or the central world of the universe. But it will sometime rise from its chrysalis enfoldments, and come into conscious life and activity. In this life of sense, we have taken our journey into a far country away from our Father's house or the realm of pure spirit. "Our (true) country," says Plotinus (that is, truly existing being), "is that from whence we came, and where our Father lives." Again, he says of this world of spirit, the kingdom of God in man, "Whoever is a spectator of this divine world becomes at one and the same time both the spectator and the spectacle, for our inmost self and immortal *Ego* is inseparable from it. He no longer beholds this intelligible world, or world of intelligence, externally, but he becomes the same with it." (*Plotinus*, Translated by Thomas Taylor, p. 100.) This is man as an image or idea of God, and not the vulgar and debased thing to which that divine name is usually given. And faith, when it rises above mere opinion, and becomes a clear intellectual perception of eternal truth, is the divinest power and highest saving and healing energy in the universe. "If thou canst believe, all things are possible to him that believeth." (Mark ix: 23.) "If ye had faith as a grain of mustard, ye might say to this sycamore tree, Be thou plucked up by the root, and be thou planted in the sea, and it would obey you." (Luke xvii: 6.) This is a sober truth, and not an Oriental exaggeration. The attainment of true faith is the recovery of the lost *magic word*. It is a perception of eternally existing realities, and is the Logos (or Word) in man. It is what Paul denominates, "the word of faith." Sin, in the Platonic sense of error, illusion, false opinion, is the opposite of faith, for "whatsoever is not of faith is sin." (Rom. xiv: 23.) But faith is not merely intellectual light; it is conjoined with love or feeling. Says Swedenborg, "All who are in the truths of faith from good are in power from the Lord, and this in the degree that they attribute all power to Him and none to themselves." (*Arcana Celestia*, 4932.) This is Paul's paradox. "When I am weak, then am I strong." (II Cor. xii: 10.) Again, "Truth has no power except from good, but its power from good is incredibly great." (*Arcana Celestia*, 6344, also 6328, 8200.) "The power of truth from good is so exceeding great, that if man were inspired by divine truth from the Lord, he would have the strength of Samson." (*Arcana Celestia*, 10,182.)

In the Kabalistic scheme of emanation, called the Ten Sephiroth, or universal outflowing divine principles, which correspond to something in man, the fourth is love, and has as a corresponding name of God, *El*, meaning the Strong God, the Mighty One. The fifth, which is justice or faith, has, as a corresponding name of God, *Eloah*, the Almighty. The two together make the *Elohim*, the creative potencies mentioned in the first chapter of Genesis as forming the world. The fifth Sephira or emanation is also called *strength*, and the fourth *greatness*, because love enlarges the sphere of our life and our sympathies, while a man is little in proportion as he is selfish. Faith was also called by the Kabalists the right hand of God, and love the left hand. This gives us a sublime view of the power of faith, as it is a manifestation of the divine nature in man, and explains the words of Jesus, "Have the faith of God." (Mark xi: 22.) The author of the Epistle to the Hebrews asserts that God created the worlds (*Æons*) by faith. (Heb. xi: 3.) As the Logos, it is the creative potency in man.

As to the faith of which Jesus speaks, let it be observed, that a seed signifies a spiritual truth, a living *idea*. The seed of the woman, that is, the truths of wisdom, the Divine Sophia, shall bruise the serpent's head, — the serpent signifying the principle of sense, the *Nephesh*, with its illusions and fallacies. "For, as Moses lifted up the serpent in the wilderness, even so must the son of man (or the soul) be lifted up," and it must be done on the cross, which represents the union of the intellect with the love or feeling.

The proper ground of faith is the divine *promise*. But what is meant by this? There is often a deep spiritual philosophy concealed beneath the external envelope of a name or word, as has been taught in the "Cratylus" of Plato, which is a dialogue on the rectitude of names. The name of a thing expresses its inward essence and true nature and quality. The word "promise" is from the Latin *promissum*, and means a thing sent beforehand, and in this sense answers to the Greek word. It is, as it were, the preëxistent *idea* of a certain good announced beforehand, and which waits to be recognized and appropriated by faith, and then it becomes an actuality or a thing possessed. The divine promises are based on the inseparable and immutable connection of certain things with each other, as substance and form, cause and effect. There are some things that God has so joined together that they can never be put asunder. If we have one, we must have the other. There are certain mental conditions of such a nature, and so indissolubly associated, that if I have the one, I must and surely will have the other. This may be illustrated by the fixed laws of geometry. If we make a triangle, the value of all the angles is just two right angles, neither more nor less. If we make a triangle with lines composing it of any length, and we are asked, What is the sum of its angles? we can always say, with absolute certainty, two right angles. This we knew beforehand, for it is based upon the immutable truth and reality of things. Now the promises of God are the announcement of certain eternal truths, and their divinity consists in their truth, and not in the book where they are found. They are divinely and unalterably true wherever they are found, whether in the Vedas, the Bible, the Koran, or the Almanack, or by whomsoever announced. This is forcibly asserted by Paul when he says that the promises of God are Yea and Amen (from the Hebrew *Amuna*, truth), in Christ Jesus, unto the glory of God by us (II Cor.

i : 20) ; that is, they are the announcement of certain eternal truths, like the affirmation that if you make a triangle, you have, and must have from the essential nature of things, two right angles, and this result is given beforehand, so that you need not stop to count or measure the angles. The intuitive perception of these eternal truths is faith. If we are governed by the body and the senses, or walk after the flesh, as Paul would say, we shall be sick and die. Our existence will be a dying life and living death. But, if we are governed by the spirit, and believe the spirit and disbelieve the body and the senses, we shall live, and greatly live. This, in a word, is faith.

Jesus affirms that if we *ask*, we receive, not that we shall sometime receive. This is eternally true, and faith is the recognition of its truth. For asking, where it is the expression of *desire*, is receiving; for the desire is the incipiency of that which is its object, and in proportion as we *believe*, we have. The two things go together, so that every one who asks, receives, and the statement of this eternal law of the necessary conjunction of the two things is what is meant by the word promise or the sending beforehand of a thing. The promise is the expression of the *idea* of the good we seek. To add to this the element of *feeling*, makes it a living and conscious reality. Hence Jesus says, — and in his words there is the promise of God, or the announcement of an immutable truth in the heavens above and the earth beneath, — " Whatsoever things ye desire, when ye pray, believe that ye receive, and ye shall have." (Mark xi : 24.) For we have, and mentally appropriate and possess a thing, in proportion as we believe. We cannot have, unless we believe we have. These go together like substance and form, cause and effect, thought and existence. We cannot have the one without the other, and if we have the one, we must of necessity have the other.

Again, Jesus says, " Whatsoever ye shall ask the Father

in my name, he will give you." (John xvi: 23.) God gave to Jesus the name that is above every name, that at the mention of this mysterious name every knee should bow, of things in the heavens, and the earth, and under the earth. It is the name, as the Chaldean Oracles say, which rushes through the infinite worlds. Now this name is that which expresses the Christ, the crown and summit of manifested being. *That name is in us*, and represents our inmost spirit, the Son of God, and the Christ within. To ask in the name of Christ, is to ask from this summit of our being. This is in the *quality* of the Christ, and asking here is praying for that which we know to be his *desire* and *necessary impulse* to impart, and what he would ask, and does in that sense ask, the Father to give. Our inmost spirit is the Son of God in us, and the Father always hears the Son. The desire of the Christ to bless and impart good, real and not apparent good merely, may be represented by a musical note or sound. Our asking from the Christ realm of our being, is a note in harmony with it, and the two blend together in one sound, and as such it reaches the all-hearing ear of the listening God, the supreme and eternal Goodness.

APPENDIX.

THE PRAYER OF FAITH THAT SAVES THE SICK, OR THE HEALING POWER OF SPIRITUAL TRUTH.

IT is a principle taught in the spiritual philosophy of all ages and countries that prayer is the most intense form of the action, or influence, of one mind upon another. All genuine prayer is a union of intellect and feeling, and this makes it a *living* spiritual force. It is thought vivified by love, and directed toward its object. As the will is the primal force in man, and is but the intensifying and focalization of desire, the highest effort of will naturally takes the form of silent invocation. It spontaneously seeks to gain a higher level, a mightier strength to lean upon, and union with a Life that can lift us from our own and rescue us from the weakness of an isolated individuality. It is confirmed and perfected by *faith*, which, as both Plato and Jesus teach, is an operative spiritual *cause;* and the will, combined with faith, goes forth more in the form of affirmation than that of supplication. As Jesus — who is himself the way, and the truth, and the life — affirms that whatsoever we ask the Father in his *name*, or in the quality of the Christ, the supreme Wisdom, the Father will give us; and as our own *spirit* is the Christ in us, and is one with Him, we use the following *formula* as expressing the highest activity of the *will, faith,* and *imagination*, in an act of *benediction*, or the communication of good and truth to others, and as a vehicle through which God's "saving health" — which is the interior meaning of the name Jesus — may be imparted to the souls of men. The apostles declare that it was by the saving virtue of the *name* of Jesus that the cripple at the Beautiful gate of the temple was healed, and that there is none other *name* under heaven given among men whereby we must be saved. (Acts iv: 12.) According to a law of correspondence, a name signifies and expresses an inward essence, principle, and quality. When the name of a person, as Washington, Napoleon, or Lincoln, is mentioned, there comes into thought the particular quality and character of the man. Hence the name represents that inward quality. The same is true of things. Their names signify to us their inward essence. The Hebrew name for Jesus (Yehoshua), as Reuchlin demonstrated in his work on the Kabala, by leaving out one letter (the *Shin*), becomes the mysterious *Yava*, the sacred and ineffable name of God among the Jews. The *Yava* (or *Yaho*) is the second Sephira, — the Sophia, or Supreme Wisdom-Principle, — and is the perfect conjunction of the intellect and the love on the highest spiritual plane. This is exactly the characteristic of Jesus and the quality of his life, and consequently is that which his name signifies. In the following prayer of faith, there is, we sincerely believe, the saving, healing virtue, of the *name* of Jesus Christ the Nazaraion, and of the principle his name represents.

INVOCATION.

In that mysterious and sovereign name that is above every name, and which signifies and represents the only *saving* principle in the universe, and before which every knee bows, in heaven, and on earth, and under the earth, and from the summit of our triune nature, and the spiritual crest of our own being, we approach in thought the Universal Presence of the Father, the one and only Life, and Supreme Reality. In thy light we recognize the truth that our *spirit* is a manifestation and personal limitation of the grand unity of Spirit, and in its essence is divine, and included in the being of

Him who is the *Crown* of all manifested existence, and the head of all principality and power, and the supreme source and inmost spring of all saving and healing influence. In our inmost and true existence and *real self*, we are not, and cannot be, diseased, for we are one with Thee. Thou wilt cause the light and power of this great truth to penetrate the darkness of our souls, and disperse the errors, and illusions, and false opinions, and deceptive appearances of our irrational and sensuous mind, the only seat of evil, and Thou wilt enable us to see and *feel* that, as immortal and divine spirits, we are well and happy, and in this region of our being, we share the deep tranquillity of the Christ and thine own eternal calm. Thou art speaking anew to us, and *in* us the creative Word, the still small voice, "Let there be light," and the darkness and blindness of the soul and of sense are becoming pierced with the radiance of a celestial day, and Thou art reducing the chaos of our lower soul to the divine order of the Spirit. We are not projecting our voiceless language of adoring and supplicating thought into vacancy, but into thy Presence, from which we cannot escape; and the ineffable light of thy Life is opening and demolishing the thick wall of solid darkness which has hitherto enclosed us. From this higher position and diviner altitude of thought, to which Thine abounding *grace* has raised us, we perceive that our true being has not been invaded by disease or any discomfort, but as included in the Christ, the Universal Spirit, is secure from all evil, and free from all sin. By the light of thy Word in us, which is the fountain of all spiritual intelligence, we perceive that our salvation in spirit and in the Christ is not to be viewed as an event which is to transpire in a distant or near future, but is to be apprehended and appropriated by *faith* as a fact existing in the present, and an eternal reality. With the humble boldness which this divine truth gives us, we view ourselves therefore as now well, and already saved in the Christ, who is in the bosom of the Father, and we with Him and *in* Him are sheltered in the secret place of the Most High, and here, overbrooded by the Infinite Life and Love, sickness and sorrow, pain and death, and the disquieting fear of them, can never reach us. Thou wilt cause us to feel more and more the divine redeeming power, and healing efficacy of this eternal truth, and the saving virtue of the *name* of Jesus; and Thou art translating this true *idea* of man and our high calling of God in Christ into a bodily expression in us, that we may be saved to the uttermost, and from the centre to the material circumference of our existence. Awaken in us all the slumbering life of the Spirit; rend from our inner eye more fully the veil of illusion; remove from our mental vision the bandage of sense; and free us from the dominion of the dull mass of the body, and the limitations and thraldom of our material being. Break every link in the fetters of our soul; remove the bars from the doors of our prison; open wide the windows of our soul to the radiance of the spiritual sun, and the true light of life will penetrate and illuminate the gloom of our disordered condition. This sublime truth, that as a *spirit* created into thine image, and indissolubly included in thine own being, we are exempt from disease and all evil, is a ray in us of thine own intelligence, and is inseparable from thine Infinite Mind and, as such, partakes of thine own tranquil and saving omnipotence. To this fixed stake we would forever cling, though assailed by doubt and fear, and tossed by storm and flood. In the name of the Christ, in whom and through whom our life is hid in Thee, the Universal Father, and only true Being, we affirm by *faith* in opposition to blind sense, that we are now freed from our infirmity. By the light and sovereign authority of the inner Word, we disown and renounce disease and sin as any part of our *immortal and real self*, and before the tribunal of the righteousness of faith, or divine rectitude of thought, we execute judgment upon them, and separate them from us in our conception as something external and foreign to our true being. *It is done.* As to all that which constitutes our permanent and unalterable personality, we are not diseased, but are now saved in Thee. And we commit the keeping of our souls unto Thee, the God of peace, who canst save us *wholly*, and preserve our *spirit* and *soul* and *body* as a harmonious unity, unto the full revelation of the light and life of immortality. "Faithful is He who calleth us, who also will do it." We trust henceforth thy boundless Wisdom, Love, and Power, to give thine own *idea* of man a full expression in us. In the name of the Christ. Amen.

When we can grasp the meaning, and measure and weigh the full import of this formula of faith, and it becomes in us a fixed mode of thought, and we can repeat it, not as a succession of empty words, but in the interior light of their deep significance, we are put in possession of the power of the inner Word, and the Spirit through which Jesus healed disease, and cast out demons. Spiritual thought can *penetrate* where spoken words can never reach, for thought is a more real force than sound. It is an *arrow* that never falls short of the mark, or misses its aim. It is the same "Spirit of truth" which brooded over the original *chaos* or unparticled and unorganized cosmic matter, and changed it into the *cosmos*, a word which primarily signifies order and arrangement. It is the same as the power of the Highest (or Divine Inmost) that overshadowed Mary. In our patients, and in every human being, there is the latent germ, the spiritual *ovum*, the dormant but still living *idea* of man in perfect health and blessedness. Spiritual thought, the light of true intelligence, united with feeling, is the Divine Sophia, the creative Wisdom-Principle and potency, which can "brood over" (or incubate, as the original word means) this latent idea in man, vivify it into consciousness, and impregnate it with a divine vitality. The repetition in thought, or in a tacit verbal utterance of something like the above form of invocation, is one of the most effectual modes of doing this. Its influence will come upon the patient like the *dew* of heaven (the old symbol of spiritual truth) upon a withering flower. The greatest forces in the universe are silent. The light of the sun falls in stillness upon the earth, and lifts countless millions of plant-germs up toward the heavens, and slowly but surely elevates the trees of the forest into the embrace of the sky. The cure of mental and bodily maladies by the influence (that is, as the word means, the *inflowing*) of one mind upon or into another, is no new thing in the world. It is not a new invention or discovery, but a rediscovery. It is a resurrection into life of the dry bones of primitive Christianity. It is based on laws of mind as fixed, and more certain, than any of the principles of chemistry — the naturally and essentially diffusive tendency of our mental states, and the absorptive and receptive nature of the soul of a patient in a passive state, and actuated by a sincere *desire* of recovery. Under the influence of fear and unbelief, or rather misbelief, disease is both contagious and infectious. Under other and better conditions, health of mind and body is equally so, for the Supreme Goodness has not given evil the advantage over us in this respect.

CHAPTER XXIV.

PSYCHOLOGICAL TELEGRAPHY, OR THE TRANSFERENCE OF THOUGHT AND IDEA FROM ONE MIND TO ANOTHER.

It is affirmed by Swedenborg that the speaking in thought, the *cogitatio loquens*, is understood by the angels and spirits who are with man; and if that is true, then it is by no means incredible or unreasonable, that, in treating a patient near or far off in space, our spiritual thought, directed toward him, should affect his spirit. When a subject is in the magnetic state, if we ask him a question in thought, he perceives it and answers it just the same as if it was spoken to him in words. It is also a marvellous fact, but nevertheless true, that if you address him in a language that he has never learned, he still understands you as easily as he would if spoken to in his native tongue; for he understands the thought and idea, which are the living soul of all language. But magnetism adds no new power to human nature. A person in a passive, and consequently impressible, state, may be influenced by our thoughts. When we use the formula of invocation given in a preceding lesson, the spiritual sphere of our minds may dispel the sphere of the patient's mind, and our thought may affect him somewhat as it would if he thought the same. It is affirmed by Swedenborg that such methods were used by the ancient Magi and the Jewish prophets, in order to excite in the minds of others a better state of thought and feeling.

The communication of thought and ideas from one mind to another without the use of spoken words, and that at great distances, has been practised in all ages of the world by the spiritually unfolded man. In Lord Lytton's "Zanoni" it is said, that, when Zanoni visits the abode of the recluse who had been his teacher, "years long and many had flown away since they met last, at least bodily and face to face. But if they are sages, thought can meet thought, and spirit meet spirit, though oceans divide the forms. Death itself divides not the wise." (*Zanoni*, Chap. V.)

Such communication is perfectly natural and easy to the spiritual man. It has been from the remotest ages, and still is practised by the Hindu adepts in occult science. Says an intelligent investigator of the phenomena exhibited by them: "Though it may seem to us a very amazing and impossible thing to sit still at home and impress our thoughts upon the mind of a distant friend by an effort of will, a Brother (an adept), living in an unknown Himalayan retreat, is not only able to converse as freely as he likes with any of his friends who are initiates like himself, in whatever part of the world they may happen to be, but would find any other modes of communication, such as those with which the crawling faculties of the outer world have to be content, simply intolerable in their tedium and inefficiency." (*The Occult World*, by A. P. Sinnett, pp. 32, 33.)

This is done in perfect harmony with the laws of spirit, and with as much ease as we can carry on a conversation with our friends in the same room with us, for what men call the supernatural is the natural in the spiritual sphere. Thought is the most *real* thing in the universe, and when united with love or emotion is the divinest and most far-reaching and penetrating force in the whole realm of being. On this subject Madam Blavatsky, a very competent witness, as she is herself an adept in the practice of psychological telegraphy, says in her great work, "Isis Unveiled," "Experiments with the telephone prove that the human voice and the sounds of instrumental music may be conveyed along a telegraphic wire to a great distance. The Hermetic philosophers taught that the disappearance from sight of a flame does not imply its actual extinction (nor indeed of the object burned). It has only passed from the visible to the invisible world, and may be perceived by the inner sense of vision, which is adapted to the things of that other and more real universe. The same rule applies to sound. As the physical ear discerns the vibrations of the atmosphere (or æther) only up to a certain point, not yet definitely fixed, but varying with the individual, so the adept, whose interior hearing has been developed, can take the sound at this vanishing point, and hear its vibrations in the *astral light indefinitely*. He needs no wires, helices, or sounding-boards; his will-power is all sufficient. Hearing with the spirit, time and distance offer no impediments, and so he may converse with another adept at the antipodes with as great ease as though they were in the same room."

"Fortunately we can produce numerous witnesses to corroborate our statement, who, without being adepts at all, have, nevertheless, heard the sound of aerial music and of the human voice when neither instrument nor speaker were within thousands of miles of the place where we sat. *In their case they actually heard interiorly, though they supposed their physical organs of hearing alone were employed.* The adept had, by a single effort of will-power, given them for the brief moment the same perception of the *spirit* of sound as he himself constantly enjoys." (*Isis Unveiled*, vol. ii., pp. 605, 606.)

These phenomena are absolutely established facts, and contain a principle which is applicable to communication with the universal world of spirit, the realm of angels, and heaven of the blest. In solitude and inward silence, their thoughts may come to us as "the still small voice within." What we call language is only thought expressed on the plane of sense. But our true being lies behind the veil of sense, and this may hear and speak the soundless language of thought and ideas. Thought, being the supersensuous side of language, is a more real and potent thing than spoken words. On this principle is based the practice of the cure of disease by the ideal or transcendental method.

The transmission of thought, the transference of ideas from one mind to another, in perfect harmony with the laws of mind, and without a miracle, has been practised by many persons in various countries. In this case, the old maxim of the Hindu metaphysical philosophy, and one much older than Lord Bacon, holds good: "Power belongs to him who knows." If we understand the laws that govern it, and the conditions under which it can take place, we can do it. It takes place as naturally as the descent of water from a higher to a lower level. Thought is not a faculty of mind; it is mind itself. It is the very being of mind. It is *spirit*. And our spirit may enter the soul region of another person in a passive state, as readily as the light of the sun enters a sky-light in the roof of a building and illuminates the room below.

The Abbé Fretheim, who lived in the seventeenth century and published a work entitled "Steganographie," could converse with his friends any time he pleased, by a transmission of his thoughts. He says: "I can make my thoughts known to the initiated, at a distance of many hundred miles, without word, writing, or cypher, and even without a messenger. If any correspondent should be buried in the deepest dungeon, I could still convey to him my thoughts, as frequently as I chose, and this quite simply, without superstition, without the aid of spirits." A certain Cordanus is chronicled as having been able to send his spirit or *thought-presence* on such psychological errands, with any messages he chose to transmit. When he did so, he affirms that he felt "as if a door was opened and I myself immediately passed through it, leaving the body behind me." There was more reality in this than the world at large is prepared to admit. It is not an illusion, but a substantial reality; since, by one of the deepest laws of my inner being, *the spirit is always present with the spirit of him who is the object of thought.* So wherever my thought is, there the spirit itself is; and the spirit is the sovereign power in human nature.

The case of a high German official, a counsellor Weserman, is mentioned in a German paper on Psychology, published in 1820, who claimed to be able to cause any friend or acquaintance, at any distance, to dream of any subject he chose or see any person he liked. His claims were proved good, and were testified to on several occasions, by sceptics and learned professional persons. (*Isis Unveiled*, vol. i., pp. 476, 477.)

From my own observation of these, to many incredible, phenomena, now for more than twenty years, I have no reason to doubt the truth of the above. I will only say, that all that is claimed above to have been done, I have many times witnessed. And why should it be thought a thing incredible, that there should be such a thing as a system of psychological telegraphy, and even the transference of our inner conscious self to any distance of space, which for it has no real existence? Every one knows that he can transport himself wherever he pleases by that power and mode of *thought* which we call *imagination*. But imagination is inseparable from the *spirit* of man; so that wherever I imagine myself to be, there my real personality is. And if *I* am there, why may I not speak in thought, which is the language of spirit, to my friend, who, as to his inner being, is another spirit? The thing is really as natural as our ordinary conversation with each other.

In sleep, when the soul is more or less emancipated from the body, and freed from its limitations and restraints, the mind acts with more intensity and power on other minds. And the more we can pass into an interior state, where the bodily senses become quiescent, which is the Neo-Platonic ecstasy, the more we can do so. This is well illustrated by a fact mentioned by Dr. Abercrombie, which, as an instance of psychological telegraphy, or the transfer of thought and idea from one mind to another, is explained on this principle: A young man, who was at an academy an hundred miles from home, dreamed that he went to his father's house in the night, tried the front door, but found it locked; got in by a back door, and finding nobody out of bed, went directly to the bed-room of his parents. He then said to his mother, whom he seemed to himself to find awake, "Mother, I am going a long journey, and have come to bid you good-bye." On which she answered, under much agitation, "O dear son, thou art dead!" He instantly awoke, and thought no more of his dream, until a few days after he received a letter from his father inquiring very anxiously after his health, in consequence of a frightful dream his mother had on the same night in which the dream just mentioned occurred to him. She dreamed she heard some one attempt to open the front door, then go to the back door, and at last come into her bed-room. She then saw it was her son, who came to the side of her bed, and said, "Mother, I am going a long journey, and am come to bid you good-bye"; on which she exclaimed, "O dear son, thou art dead!" Nothing unusual happened to either of the parties. (*Inquiries concerning the Intellectual Powers*, p. 210.)

Dr. Abercrombie can give no explanation of this interesting fact, though he vouches for its truthfulness. But it is neither a miracle nor a "coincidence," by which is meant the happening of two things together. But it is easily accounted for on the principle of the transmission of thought and idea, under certain conditions, from one mind to another. Once admit the possibility of this, and all is plain and natural.

I remember to have read in the *New York Tribune* many years ago, an account of two men who were intimate friends, and who, on separating from each other for a short time on business which took them many miles apart, agreed that on a certain day, at nine o'clock at night, each would retire to his room and think of the other, and write down their thoughts. When they met, they were to compare what they had written. One of them at the appointed time went to his room, but forgot the engagement, and retired to bed and fell asleep. The other thought of his friend, and imagined a beautiful landscape garden with flowers, arbors, fountains, statues, etc., and *wrote down his thoughts and ideas, with his mind fixed upon his friend*. On meeting, the one who forgot the appointment he had made, apologized for his forgetfulness, but said that in his sleep he had a remarkable dream, which, on waking in the morning, he had written down. On reading it, it was found in all essential particulars to be a copy of the thoughts of the other. This was not a mere "coincidence," but under the same or like circumstances would "happen" again. How much the thoughts of our friends influence us for good or evil, we do not know, but much more than the world is ready to admit. Our formula of invocation is based on the reality of this influence, and aims to show how most effectually to use it, and how our *will, imagination*, and *faith* may best employ the divine power of truth in the cure of mental and bodily disease.

The communication of thought and idea from one mind to another takes place without effort on our part, under certain conditions and limitations that are necessary to prevent its being abused to purposes of evil. It is easy for him to do who "knows," but if it were too easily done, it would introduce inextricable confusion and disorder into the realm of mind. To do it requires a certain degree of spiritual development, which, when attained, deprives one of all desire or inclination to abuse it, or to use it only for the most beneficent ends, as the relief of suffering, the removal of the cause of mental inharmony, and the cure of disease. It is only giving quality, and direction, and a definite aim to the sphere of our own thoughts and feelings, which is very easily done. Says Cornelius Agrippa: "Out of every body proceed images, indivisible substances, and on that account a man is in a condition to impart his thoughts to another man who is hundreds of miles away." (Sprengel's *History of Medicine*, Part II., p. 267. Ennemoser's *History of Magic*, Vol. II., p. 254.)

This is what Swedenborg calls the emanative sphere of a person or thing. Each emanative ray or immaterial atom is a *living resemblance* or idea of the person, possessing his peculiar quality, and by means of this sphere we may make ourselves visible to the inner senses of another person remote from us in space. This idea may take shape in the universal substance, the cosmic matter, and be, as it were, a duplicate of ourselves. It is our "thought," our inner and real personality externalized and extended abroad. According to the doctrine of Aristotle, every object and every person is continually emitting or throwing off certain resemblances of themselves. These species, or phantasms, as they were called, like the Platonic ideas, are directly present to our organs of sense in the soul, however remote in space the objects may be from which they proceed. This was the theory of vision which prevailed in Europe for more than a thousand years; and it has the merit of being as rational as the one adopted by the materialistic science of to-day.

Spirit cannot effect the grosser form of matter directly, but only through an intermediate substance or principle. In order to reach the *soul* of the patient, and through this affect the body, our spiritual thought and ideas must be impressed upon the "astral light," the universal life-principle, which is the wire through which our thought must pass. This is always near us, for every soul is in it and is a part of it. Our thought may be impressed upon it by a whispered utterance, and tacit speech, also by the hand (and this is the philosophy of gesture), and also by an *expiratory respiration*. The hand can be made the silent tongue that speaks the voiceless language of ideas. It may be made to speak a language understood by the life-principle, the world-soul, just as certainly as you can *beckon* a man to come to you, or go away from you, and without saying a word can cause him to look at an object by pointing your finger towards it. In treating a patient by the transcendental method, we must learn to talk to him in *thought*, in *words*, and with the *hand*.

When a person is in the magnetic state, what you suggest to him becomes the law of his being. Say to him that an apple is an orange, or that water is wine, and he has so vivid an idea and *belief* of those things that they are transformed into an orange, or into wine, as the case may be, possessing all the sensible properties of those objects. But only a few persons are good subjects of magnetism. Fortunately, it has been found that when a person is in a *passive* state, and is *desirous* of being healed, and is predisposed to *believe* and to follow your directions, to silently suggest the truth to him creates in him a tendency to think the same. This is a very ancient principle of the science of magnetism. There is a silent action of mind on mind, without the use of spoken words. It is generally admitted by medical men, that our faith will affect ourselves; but they wholly ignore the fact that our faith and imagination may affect another, if not to the same extent as it does ourselves, yet as certainly in a degree. We can be helpers of another man's faith. That our faith or mode of thinking may affect the mind of another, through the medium of a universal mind or life which connects all minds by a law of sympathy, is a truth recognized in the promise of Jesus, "These signs shall follow them that *believe*," one of which is, "They shall lay hands on the sick, and they shall recover." (Mark xvi: 18.)

The principle of silent suggestion has its application also to self-healing. It is possible for the higher soul or spirit to speak to the lower soul somewhat as we address another person. The faith of which Paul so often speaks, and by which we attain to righteousness, or a divine rectitude of thought, is the *recognition* and *affirmation* of the truth with regard to our real self, that in the Christ or spirit we are already saved. In the Christ are hid all the treasures of wisdom and knowledge, and in him we are complete or made full. (Col. ii: 9, 10.) The intuition of this great truth, and the confident affirmation of it, is the Pauline justification, and Kabalistic righteousness, which means soundness of mind. It is a faith that makes us whole. To affirm this of ourselves in thought is a supreme act of faith. And to give it vocal or verbal utterance intensifies and confirms it. " For with the heart (or in the centre of our being), man believeth unto righteousness; and with the mouth, confession is made unto salvation." (Rom. x : 10.)

CHAPTER XXV.

RESURRECTION FROM THE BODY, OR THE LIBERTY OF THE SONS OF GOD.

ACCORDING to Plato, there was once a winged race of men on the earth. Of course this is symbolical of a race who could emancipate themselves from the limitations and thraldom of the body, and who could rise in their thoughts above the plane of sense. According to Swedenborg's science of correspondence, wings denote spiritual truths, and to rise on eagles' wings signifies to be elevated by spiritual truths to celestial light. (*Arcana Celestia*, 8764.)

The great majority of mankind have lost their wings, and are grovelling in the dust.

> "Here man, fool man, inters celestial hopes,
> Without one sigh, and prisoner of earth,
> And pent beneath the moon, here pinions all
> His wishes, winged of God to fly at infinite,
> And reach it there where seraphs gather
> Immortality on life's fair tree, fast by
> The throne of God."

The higher soul of man, imprisoned in the body and buried in the sepulchre of irrational sense, loses the use of its wings, and its angelic powers are latent and dormant. Instead of soaring into the heavens, it can at best only wade in the mud.

The true wings of the soul are faith and love, or the perception of real truth, and a pure emotional state to balance it.

How to emancipate the soul from the body and the mind from the illusions of sense, so that we may attain to a truly spiritual mode of thought and feeling, and to the almost deific powers belonging to such a condition, is the great problem of religion and philosophy. Momentous consequences are involved in its solution. The importance and necessity of the resurrection of the soul from the body in order to the attainment of a spiritual life on earth is well stated by Sokrates in the "Phædo" of Plato. He says: "In fact it is quite plain that if we are ever to know anything clearly, we must be released from the body, that the soul by itself may see things by themselves as they really are. And then only, methinks, shall we have that which we desire, and of which we call ourselves lovers, namely, wisdom." Here, then, is the only pathway which leads up to the temple of a true spiritual knowledge. For as Sokrates, or rather Plato through him, says, "We shall be so much nearer to true knowledge the more we refrain from such contact and fellowship with the body as is not absolutely necessary." The way to effect this emancipation of the soul, imprisoned in the body, from material limitations, at which all the ancient philosophies aimed, is as well stated by Sokrates in the "Phædo" as it can be expressed. He says: "They who love knowledge know that their soul when first received by philosophy is absolutely bound up in the body and glued fast to it, and compelled to survey the things that *really exist* through it as through the bars of a dungeon, and not in her own nature; and that she is wallowing in all ignorance as in a mire, and is not aware that the strength of her prison comes from her own *desires*, so that the prisoner actually conspires to his own captivity."

"Well, as I said, lovers of knowledge know that philosophy, receiving the soul in this condition, gently encourages her, and tries to effect her release by showing that perception by means of the eyes and ears and other senses is altogether deceitful, persuading her, moreover, to withdraw the senses so far as she can dispense with them, and exhorting her to retire into herself and be self-collected, and to believe none other than herself, and that part of real independent existence which she contemplates directly in herself; but to hold as untrue whatever things, by means of different faculties, she may perceive to be varying in their different manifestations; knowing that such as these belong to the visible and to the realm of sense, but that what she sees in herself alone belongs to the invisible and to the realm of thought. She withdraws herself as much as possible from pleasures, and desires, and pains, and fears, deeming that when any one is powerfully affected by pleasure, or fear, or grief, or desire, he brings upon himself no slight evil, as might be expected, like sickness, or waste of property, occasioned by indulging the passions, but he suffers the last and worst of all evils, and yet takes no account of it."

"And what is that evil? It is this. The soul of every man at the time of undergoing intense joy or intense sorrow is led to believe that whatever causes these is most real and true, although in reality it is not so. And this applies especially to things visible. And it is in this state of feeling that the soul is most effectually imprisoned in the body. Because every pleasure and every pain is, as it were, a nail which nails and clamps the soul to the body, and fashions her in the image of the body, causing her to believe that to be true which the body affirms to be true, and from agreeing with the body and rejoicing in what appertains thereto, she must perforce, I think, end by acquiring a like nature and habits." (*Phædo*, sec. 83.)

These are golden words, uttered by one who represents the ancient wisdom, the old wine of the kingdom of God. We need to learn to close the senses to the external world of illusion, and turn the mind inward towards the light of the unseen and real world. We must forever fix it in our minds that things seen by the senses are temporal, unreal, and evanescent shadows, but things not seen by the mortal eye, but lying wholly beyond its ken, are the only eternal and enduring realities. We must as much as possible divest the soul, the inner man, of all its material and sensuous integuments, "the coats of skin" with which it has been clothed, and free it from the finite limitations of its personal existence, and leave it in its primitive innocent nakedness to absorb the light and life of "true being," and to become one with that boundless realm of uncreated spiritual effulgence. We must close the lower windows, and, like the ancient temples, let the light in at the top. Then

> "The world that time and sense have known
> Falls off, and leaves us God alone."

It is a fundamental doctrine of the Hermetic philosophy that the soul of man is not of necessity included in the body, nor bounded and circumscribed by it. The body exists in the soul, and is included in its existence, but the body does not and cannot limit and contain the soul. This is the divine method of viewing it, and is in direct contradiction to the common popular conception of it. According to Plato in the "Timæus," God first creates the world-soul, the *anima mundi*, and then the world is created or generated in it. The world-soul is not limited by the world, but fills all space, and is space itself, in which everything exists. So the soul of man, according to the Platonic philosophy, was made out of the universal soul, of which it is a personal and finite limitation, and in the interior of the soul the body was formed. The body, to use an imperfect illustration and analogy, is like an island in a lake or ocean. While it is true that the island is pervaded by the water, it does not contain, measure, or bound it. He who views the body as containing the soul is like the man who should suppose that the water he finds by digging in the sand of an island is all there is in the lake or ocean which surrounds it. So the soul of man is much more than what is included in the body. It is by divine right a freeman of infinitude, as it is not, only in our unbelief or misbelief, separated and disjoined from the divine soul of the universe. This is a principle of the ancient wisdom, and is one of far-reaching importance. When the soul is freed from the bondage of the enfeebling conception that it is *in* the body, its fetters are broken, and the stone is removed from the door of its sepulchre. It is no longer subject to the body, which is an inverted order of its life, but it becomes its rightful sovereign. If the body is not external to the soul, but is internal, then the soul, being more than the body, when properly instructed and reinforced by the higher divine spirit, can form the body after the pattern of any *idea* it pleases. Men on the stage form an idea of a certain state which they would represent, and even children in their sports do this, and then the idea moulds the body into its outward expression. Can we not make these bodily representations of an inward idea permanent? We can *become* the part we play. In the drama of life we can assume the character of perfect health, and the body will come into harmony with that idea. For the body is passive and inert clay, and the soul is the potter. That the soul is not of necessity imprisoned in the body like a bird in a cage, but as a part of the divine Soul of the world, from which it is never sundered, may attain to a boundless freedom, with its senses almost unlimited in their range, is a truth which has always been known to the initiates of the inner sanctuary. This is the liberty of the "sons of God," of which Paul speaks, and which is enjoyed by the adepts of the Himalaya Mountains to-day. A soul imprisoned in the body is subject to the laws of matter; freed from the body, it is subject only to the laws of thought.

But how reach this state? Not as long as the soul is bound to matter, and views matter and the body as *really existing things*. Not surely as long as the soul thinks and feels that it is limited to the body and bounded by it. For then its powers are dormant, and it can act only in and through the body. On this subject let the soul in us listen to the voice of the ancient wisdom. Says Plotinus (*Ennead* 3, lib. 6), "Since matter is neither soul, nor intellect, nor life, nor form, nor reason, nor bound, but a certain indefiniteness; nor yet capacity, for what can it produce? Since it is foreign from all these, it cannot merit the appellation of being, but is deservedly called non-entity." He proceeds to affirm that it is but the shadow and imagination of bulk, like an image in a mirror or in water. It is constituted in the shade and defect of true being, and hence must be the most unreal thing in the universe, a mere flying and ever-changing mockery. It has, in fact, no solidity, which is one of the most firmly seated of our illusions in regard to it, and one of the last to quit its hold upon us. For when a man puts his hand upon a block of marble, it is difficult to feel that its solidity is only a sensation of resistance in us. So of all its so-called properties. Supposing those sensations to be all removed from the soul, with their removal, all matter, and hence also the human body, is gone. And whenever those modifications of mind or sensations exist in us, then matter exists, for it is nothing else.

Plotinus also says "that those who view body as a real being, and make sense the standard and measure of truth, are affected like persons in a dream, who imagine that the perceptions of sleep are true. For sense is alone the employment of the dormant soul; *since as much of the soul as is merged in the body, so much of it sleeps.* But true elevation and true wakefulness are a resurrection from, and not with, the dull mass of the body. For indeed a resurrection with the body is only a transmigration from sleep to sleep, and from dream to dream, like a man passing in the dark from bed to bed." (*Introduction to the Timæus*, by Thomas Taylor, p. 431.) In the light of this Neo-Platonic philosophy, with what fulness of meaning come the words of Paul to us: "Awake to *righteousness* and *sin* not" (1 Cor. xv: 34), where righteousness is used for the Kabalistic *right thinking* or faith, and sin for the illusions of sense. He also says, "Awake thou that sleepest (or thou that art sunk in the life of sense), and arise from the dead, and the Christ shall give thee light." (Eph. v: 14.) There is no other way to the attainment of true spiritual life, light, and power.

www.ingramcontent.com/pod-product-compliance
Lightning Source LLC
Chambersburg PA
CBHW030107170426
43198CB00009B/525